DON'T JUDGE a DICK by ITS FORESKIN

DON'T JUDGE a DICK by ITS FORESKIN

God, Life & REVOLUTION

MAX GOLD

DON'T JUDGE a DICK by ITS FORESKIN

Both fan mail and hate mail should be addressed to the author and mailed to the publisher at the following address:

Four Corner Press
224 5th Ave, Ste. 1813
New York, NY 10001
USA

Alternatively, please try: max@dont-judge-a-dick-by-its-foreskin.com

Max uses Microsoft Word, Quark XPress 8.0, Bic Reaction™ and Paper Mate® gel pens.

LCCCN: 69-6969-69696

ISBN: 978-0-692-01117-1

MOTIVATION

Bill Hicks, Allen Carr, Alice in Chains, Dominic Cifarelli, Classical Composers, Joseph Campbell, Larry David, Deftones, Chris Farley Milton Friedman, Jimi Hendrix, Father Christopher Hartley, Carl Jung, Lenny Kravitz (when he had dreds), Timothy Leary, Seth MacFarlane, Jim Morrison, Nine Inch Nails, Nirvana, Trey Parker, Neil Peart, Rage Against the Machine, Ayn Rand, Joe Rogan, Sevendust, Slash, Smashing Pumpkins, Soundgarden, Doug Stanhope, Matt Stone, System of a Down, Jean Vanier,

Tool

FUCK YOU

The flakes, the starfuckers, the cockblockers, the people up in the rafters in life, the envious

THANK YOU

Dad and Mom, Mosy, Charl, Sly Si, Lesley and Kees, Blonde sister, friends, parents of friends, the Bellhouse and Vidal families, Luke, Brucey, “Officer St. Clair,” everyone associated with 3F on 77 East. 12th St., Aunt Kay, Benny, Emma, Robin, Reed, Stevie-G, Jose Louis Huerta, Cue ball and Lynette, RJ, Corcky, G, Paul A. Motherfucking Fler, Tyler & Adrienne, anyone who ever gave me a break, the many strangers and the awesome conversations, Lauren and any woman who ever...

CONTENTS

ACT I

CONTENTS CONTINUED

MORE CONTENTS

EVEN MORE CONTENTS

ADDITIONAL CONTENTS

ACT II

YOU GUESSED IT

LASTLY

ACT I

XIII
DEATH.

READ THIS FIRST

Honestly, I hate the introductions to books. They're like a national anthem before a game or previews before a movie; unessential to the experience, easily forgotten, and plugging something you didn't show up for. But an introduction is needed here if you're going to read on with any sense of purpose.

This is a book for people who like shooting the shit, learning more about life, having a few laughs, and who are going through harder times for any number of the reasons out there. This is probably not a book for people who schedule their lives around watching *Jersey Shore* or subscribe to *People* magazine. But, this is not a work that you have to read from beginning to end.

It's a book of philosophy and ideas that help promote the individual and one of the few places that protects the individual the most – The United States of America. Almost every topic that can ignite a bar brawl gets ample attention here. Because of its encyclopedic-like structure and the girth of subjects covered, feel free to read any part of the book in whatever order you'd like.

For instance, you could start by reading the bibliography and try to find the secret chapter that's cryptically embedded within it. Or you could read up on taxes while having a cigarette. Breeze through the page devoted to drugs while you're taking a dump. Skim through the topic of sex while on the subway and learn how a woman showing a picture to her boyfriend, of herself blowing another man, can actually amount to some good in the long run. Why not read the part on Muslims that's typed in reverse, right-to-left, for kicks? Why not distinguish the difference between psychopaths and sociopaths while you're in a waiting room? Flip through the part on immigration, which even offers a Spanish translation. Find out what God is while enjoying a cold beer. There's something appealing in here for everyone.

And the best part is (cue the tympani orchestra drums)... not one section of this book takes more than five minutes to read; most take about a minute or two. It gets on with it so you can as well.

When you're finished you'll know a little more about yourself and you just might want to talk about America, how it provides the ideal environment for you to be who and what you are, and help reverse the tide of sewage washing up on it lately. With any luck, you'll help start a revolution.

There's the intro. Good luck and word to your mother.

WHO BREASTFED ADAM?

What is God? I roll my eyes at the mention of the topic or word God, just as much as the next guy, but keep an open mind here for just a second. A lot of the problems that people have with one another, and within themselves, are a result of not knowing the answer to this question. We don't realize what it's all about.

Sure there are "answers," but they're not the right ones - the true ones. And because they're not right and true we don't believe in them; we can't accept them and identify with them in our hearts. And so we live on in doubt, overly vulnerable, because we don't even know who, what, how, and why any of us are; let alone ourselves. We go through life winging it, hoping to get by as best we can.

If we knew what God really was, we'd want to know and do more in life, and we'd be, not to sound too gay, nicer with everyone including ourselves. And I'd bet we'd treasure what we do have, all the more.

With the use of syllogism and the Lego™ building block basics of physics, we're going to discover how the human species, the universe and every other thing in it cannot be the creation of a superior being. We will prove and see just who and what this elusive God really is.

WHO BREASTFED EVE?

God is usually defined as the creator of all that is. But what is God? What is it made of? What made it? To know is to know what we are.

Here's your answer: Energy. Everything in the universe is made of the stuff and everything requires energy to be made. Stars, galaxies, a lunchbox, your cell phone, your skin – it's all comprised of energy in the form of matter.

If this all-creating God has a thinking mind, or the ability to choose and want to do things, that means it has consciousness. Consciousness is awareness of one's self and one's surroundings. If God was the first thing to ever exist and made everything thereafter, that means God would have to have existed before energy. But you see, consciousness is an extremely complex form of energy; it's energy put together to form the complex thing that is, in this instance, consciousness.

Simply put: no energy = no consciousness, but, conversely, no consciousness = there's still energy somewhere. As such, it is impossible for something that doesn't exist, to willingly decide to create itself – which is essentially, and absurdly, what every Alpha & Omega backed religion claims is the case.

Consciousness is intelligence. And if consciousness has to be made from energy and energy, as a fact, comes before consciousness, then, well, if there is something that intentionally made us and the universe it could not have made itself – it was made from energy. It is energy. It is a simple fact that consciousness cannot precede the unconscious, basic form of energy – the thing that gives birth to consciousness.

So even if we were created by an all-powerful being, that being was born of energy and cannot claim to be the creator of everything; at least not itself and, as such, isn't the highest power.

IF THEY WERE BORN AS ADULTS, WERE THEY REALLY HUMAN?

COMMON QUESTIONS:

Q 1: But what if there's a guy out there not made of energy, but made out of something entirely different, who made our universe with his own private stash of energy?

A: Following the same paradigm as described in the last few paragraphs, the guy didn't create himself before he even existed, so he's not that omnipotent. Lastly, the guy's decision to create a universe is evidence of consciousness; which means he is MADE of energy.

Q 2: But what if the God that many religions attest to created energy and this God is comprised of something other than energy?

A: If so, why did he have to stop and rest on the seventh day of creation? Was he low on energy? How can the source of everything be lacking something at a given point in time? Again, this doesn't matter because, still, any being that is conscious could not have consciously or intentionally created itself before the conception of consciousness and concept of intention ever existed, as many religions attest to.

Q 3: Could there be something out there that creates energy; the energy that eventually turns into universes?

A: For sure. But it would be doing so as part of an unconscious system. That said, if this were the case I suppose that something conscious could learn to harness or manipulate this "thing's" ability to create energy, but this is hypothetical masturbation. While we're there though, I suppose it has to be possible for a conscious entity to learn how to create more energy, even though as it stands now – energy can't be created; even then, anything created by this entity would be no less inferior in technical terms as it would be cut from the same cloth, both literally and figuratively speaking (as we will see shortly*).

DID ANY OF THEIR GRANDCHILDREN HAVE BIRTH DEFECTS FROM THE INBREEDING?

This is all good, but what is energy? Energy is the capacity to do work. Energy is what is needed to do work; so work is something that needs energy to be done. The act or concept of creating is work and something that requires energy. But here is where it gets tricky. Anything that is manifest (physically perceived) is called matter. And matter is energy. Matter is just energy in a condensed, more complex form; hence the e=mc squared bullshit that most of us have heard of, but can't even begin to explain.

Our planet, the things in and on it, and ourselves included are all energy formed into different bits of matter. *Because all life and matter is energy and energy is God, we are a part of God.

Not the God, just a part of it. And because we are the most intelligent component of this planet, we are akin to the mind of God; individuals who comprise a whole, experiencing life (energy/God/ourselves) subjectively; each individual's mind akin to a neuron in the brain of God.

But what made energy? No one really knows. As hard as it may be to think that from nothing can come something, it's a possibility. The laws of physics state that energy cannot be created and cannot be destroyed. All of the energy present in the universe today equals the same amount as when it was first created. What this law can reveal, though, is that because we are comprised of energy, although our consciousness may be destroyed upon death, our basic essence cannot be, because you cannot destroy energy; it merely transfers from state to state.

In any event, there you have it: Energy, as far as humans and other matter in the universe are concerned, is God. Energy was, and is, used to create everything in the universe. Everything manifest in the universe is comprised of energy. *We are energy.*

SO WHAT?

We, and everything around us, are made of the same stuff that creates everything, everywhere - energy. Even if you believe that we were intentionally made by something, we are equal to it in that we share the same life source, just as a puppy does with us. Any one of those three things (your God, us, or the puppy) are equal in the eyes of the universe; any attempt to make one more important than the other is a matter of subjective rationale (although if a person or a puppy were hanging off a cliff and I only had one rope and one chance to toss it, the puppy would have to hope for a branch or a root on the way down).

Our life source wasn't "given to us." It was made unconsciously. If you want to believe in an omnipotent God, that's your choice. But we can say that there isn't a God who created everything that ever existed with intent. And that being the case, the God you may believe in isn't as powerful as you may claim, and, if you believe in this nonsense, he's equally related to us just the same.

Because we are all equal and free, we are all equal and free to learn and live for ourselves, using the rules and tools that work best for us. God isn't a mystery or some kind of cosmic Rubik's Cube™. It is all around us and the more we learn about our surroundings and ourselves, the more we come to know what it is. Learning, feeling, emotions, games, drugs, sex, ecologies, cities, planets, galaxies... and anything imaginable are all a part of the thing that makes up God. There's nothing to fear, but the people who tell you to.

*If we all woke up to this we'd realize that we are all we've got. We'd actually make being a human and living on earth as close to paradise as we could. But we don't. We go on repeating the same shit, while only a very few people, usually against great social odds, actually create the things that help make life better. And only a very few of us live the lives we choose to. We're here, we're it, and it doesn't matter what happens when we're gone because we just get recycled into a universal compost of energy; the same compost of energy that is used to create new things later. Sadly, truth isn't easy for people to accept... it forces them to question themselves and reveals the cracks.

INTELLIGENT, IGNORANT, IGNORANT

There are three kinds of people in this world with respect to, on a basic level, intelligence. There are people who believe something at first listen, those who disbelieve something at first listen, and those who question at first listen. The first two are equally as dumb because they never get the facts in order to best determine the truth for themselves; they jump to conclusions.

But the people who question and put themselves in the middle ground where they can truly learn and discover for themselves if what they have heard, or have been shown, is fact or truth, can be said to be intelligent.

WHO ARE WE?

To really get this question we need to know what we are. We are organisms, multicellular organisms. An organism is a living thing comprised of one or more cells. A cell is a building block of life and is a life itself. The human body is a collection of cells that function to make up a functioning human body. Brain cells make up the brain, liver cells make up the liver, and so on. All the cells that make up organs in our body work with other cells that help keep them alive (e.g., blood cells). Together you have a bunch of cells that form a complex network of cells to make a human body. Think of human cells to a human body as what bricks, tiles, and shingles are to a house; if people knew this stuff a thousand years ago they'd totally lose their shit. Anyway.

There are unicellular organisms and multicellular organisms. Anything that lives and can be seen with the naked eye is multicellular. The concept behind a multicellular organism is that it has many different cells (forms of life) within it that operate in their own way that, when combined together, form a complex organism. Basically, a multicellular organism is something that has a system of different organisms within it, that depend on each other for survival and whose survival provides the higher (more complex) organism with life.

Our planet is an organism, comprised of trillions and trillions of cells that have combined to form multicellular organisms within it. This planet is a glorified host to the organisms living in and on it. Its skin and mouth are its atmosphere and its source of food is the sun. Every living thing here is an organ or a parasite of some kind. And to really expand things, our planet and our solar system are just a mini organism – a cell – relative to the body of the universe; the universe could be a cell in another larger organism.

Is it any coincidence that the strands of our DNA, the program of life that is housed in our cells, look like pictures of galaxies? Nope. Because everything is connected. We are just a small part of the picture, looking at the whole picture, trying to see where we fit into it all. It's just a really complex toy doll... you know the ones that keep getting smaller inside with every one you open... the ones people use to smuggle drugs with when they run out of condoms? And the closer you look, the more you realize that we're just cells in a big organism called God... the entire mass of energy.

So great. We're organisms. We're a complex life form comprised of many small life forms that were put together to form what we call a human. And we are programmed to eat, grow, reproduce, and evolve just as the rest of life in the universe does. And we're a microcosm of the universe; we're a universe unto ourselves. So what? That's only a part of it. Our bodies are merely a means for energy to experience and express itself in physical form; when energy can do this it is called consciousness.

If consciousness wants to do something concrete, it needs a body – a vehicle if you will. And our bodies are the best designed vehicles for consciousness to maneuver in the physical world with. Consciousness is a refined level of energy; it's energy that has the ability to be aware of itself and its surroundings.

The human body, with its unique traits like limbs, opposable thumbs and a natural computer that we refer to as a brain, is the perfect tool to exist in a physical world with because it gives us the ability to manipulate our surroundings to our liking. Our bodies, which facilitate consciousness, are the biggest prize in the universe because they allow energy/matter in the universe the opportunity to experience itself and its surroundings with less restrictions and more control than, say, a rock or a tree.

So we are a living organism that enables energy to realize it is energy and that allows this energy to have... more of an experience. And this consciousness is essentially what has been coined the soul. And your soul... well, whatever anyone wants to call it, it's just energy at the end of the day. A lot of people consider the human soul unique or more special than any other living thing. This is not so and is a subjective viewpoint. We are comprised of the exact same energy as any other living thing on this planet. The difference is the way in which our DNA is programmed and in the size and functioning of our brains. With this understanding you should consider yourself fortunate to be a human. But it's the lack of this understanding amongst humans that makes it, at times, an unfortunate thing to be human.

Consciousness has to work around certain innate laws of the body. *The physiological and psychological aspects and requirements of a human body have a huge effect on consciousness, and all three can affect one another. When these laws are better understood, a better way of life can be had.*

Anyway, that is what and who we are.

WHAT MADE US & WHY IT DOESN'T MATTER

The Big Bang made us. Physics is showing us that the Big Bang may have come out of nothing; that all of the matter in our universe came from a big fucking fluke that entailed a small bit of energy/matter blowing up. The gas stew that ensued from the bang gave life to life. All living things both big and small started off from one cell that divided into two and so on and so on. Life started in the water and moved to land.

Most people in the world believe that their God made humans as a test or an act of love. Some people believe we were made by extraterrestrial beings who fused their DNA with a lesser evolved version of modern man, to help propagate intelligence throughout the universe/universes. Seeing as how we are the only species on the planet to have the intelligence we possess, and what we've learned and achieved with it, the latter is more rational; and hey, in a few hundred years we might be colonizing space, but monkeys will still be shitting from treetops, eating bananas and playing with twigs.

As hard to imagine and as frightening as it is, we don't know for sure. All that matters is that we are here in this virtual playground we call earth and what we do while we're here. We can do whatever we want – the choice is yours.

No really, it is.

WHERE HAVE WE BEEN?

Through tough times, that's where.

The human story is like that of a person. Relative to a baby, our species is coming into adolescence. We started off small, confused, and struggled for survival and comfort. The first humans dwelled in caves and ate what they could; with food scarce, no medicine, and predators all around, life expectancy was short.

The ability to express our thoughts manifested with language. With words that were understood by all to mean specific things, people could work better together, they could strategize; they could communicate. And with opposable thumbs they could manipulate objects better than any living thing, save for, maybe, a monkey. But with language it was possible for society to begin; a group of people with shared morals, tradition, culture, you name it – all because they could agree on things because they could understand what other people felt "inside."

Somewhere down the road people learned to hunt with tools; with more food people had more kids and the tools helped to build better shelter; people lived a few more years longer. A big problem for stability was having to follow where the food was; herds have migration routes and plants grow seasonally.

Our species got out of diapers not when we learned to store food, but, rather, when we learned how to produce it at will with farming - growing crops with irrigation and herding animals. Food used to be the "oil" of our species. It fuelled our economy by allowing us to stay in one place and build more complex living quarters. With less time worrying about food we were able to grow up and start thinking about other stuff. Why? Because we are programmed to try and make life easier, we are programmed to make life meet our needs; it also makes sense, too. Our true desire is to overcome our needs and fulfill our desires. To do this, progress is required. And of course progress usually requires pain; growing pains. Pain in the development of our species always comes in the form of both brutal conquests and oppressions of people, land, ideas, and objects. Where there is pain there is ignorance and learning.

We have come from being a species that was merely a part of the food cycle to being a species that can control it and, with technology, might one day be able to remove itself from the food cycle altogether.

We have a long way to go in this story of our species... because, like some kind of strange growth pattern, only certain segments of our species are developing rapidly; others failing to adapt, and leaving themselves further and further behind as a consequence.

Every new experience in life brings about the conditions for a kind of psychological infancy. We walk through these experiences with a degree of ease, only to the extent of how well we learned to walk through previous experiences in life. Our species has been walking down a long road.

WHERE ARE WE GOING?

Though most of us are totally unaware of it, humanity has been, and is, undergoing a long process of trial and error. Trial and error, in trying to figure out how to do what we want and have what we want easier, faster, and with more consistency. The result is better medicine, communication, weapons, buildings, transportation, education, food, life spans... better everything. The point is to try and make life more comfortable; to end, or at least improve, the struggle for survival. To what end, there is no consensus.

There is a vision, as I alluded to earlier, shared by some people that states we're destined to one day take our knowledge and technology and travel in space; maybe set up shop on some far away planets. We're a long way off from this scenario, but it's more than plausible. This is why it's so important that an environment of freedom and liberty can be protected so that such a feat might just be possible and realistic one day.

UNDERSTANDING WHAT MAKES US DO WHAT WE DO

Every healthy baby that is born has unlimited potential and has a sort of software program in their brains. This software includes the automatic functioning of the body's operating systems, i.e., digestive, circulatory, respiratory, reflexes, and so on.

How fucked would it be if you had to remember to breathe or secrete insulin from your pancreas? Yes, the most important shit in life is already taken care of for you – like the need to feel hungry, thirsty, tired, pain and pleasure. If you never felt hungry or thirsty you wouldn't eat enough and drink enough and then you would die. If you never got tired you wouldn't sleep, wouldn't be alert and would end up being eaten alive or going insane. If you didn't feel pain you wouldn't avoid harmful elements and if you didn't feel pleasure you wouldn't do things that your body requires, i.e., eat, drink, sleep, and reproduce. So your brain does all of this for you - every person in the world, unless handicapped in some way, has a brain with these automated functions. The part that blows is how your body has to go about obtaining the things your brain wants in order to satiate these urges.

The brain has a series of templates for survival and existence. Call them feelings, call them emotions, call them impulses; me, I call them the basis of being an animal. Fear, anger, hate, joy, sadness, and happiness. We all experience them and they are all vital for our experience as people and for our survival. You fear something if it is a potential threat to your well-being. You get angry at something if it threatens your well-being and you need to confront it. You usually hate something that threatens you, even if there is no imminent threat. You experience joy with something that makes you feel good, or unthreatened. You should experience happiness when all your needs are met and when you are doing something that feels good.

These things are essentially emotions that we share with most forms of animal life. You're afraid of a lion eating you, just like a gazelle. You get angry at your friend when they drink your last beer without asking, like a monkey gets mad at its buddy when its buddy eats its last banana. You hate being in the cold so you put on a coat, like some birds hate the cold and fly south. You feel joy when you have fun so you play sports or go out and try to get laid, like animals lie in the shade and take naps. You get sad when you don't have what makes you happy like an animal gets sad if one of its own dies. The point is that these emotions make us get off our ass and live life.

These emotions serve animals perfectly well, because they're dumber than us. We run into trouble because our brains have more room on their hard drives for... other stuff. Animals do their thing, but, more or less, they are just a part of a food chain – essential for our survival and the survival of the planet, but they're content doing what they do, and no more, because they don't have to and they can't comprehend much more.

That extra space on our hard drives is where our advanced consciousness comes into play – and where it comes into conflict with our animalistic emotions. Our higher level of consciousness has enabled us to do more than just survive. It has allowed us as a species to create regiments of recreation and pleasure light-years beyond the imagination of any animal, e.g., sporting events and games, music, theme parks, and so on. This higher consciousness has allowed us to create machines to do work for us, to help us eat, move around, and create beyond the imagination of anyone living a hundred years ago.

But this expanded awareness is a powerful thing when it can be channeled towards serving the motives of our emotions (considering most people aren't aware of what emotions are, let alone being in control of them). We can kill people and other living things in some pretty fucked up ways. We can damage things (environment, people, property) severely in the pursuit of joy and happiness. People can think and hold destructive views in order to feel less threatened; these modes of thinking and views often ending up in harmful actions.

Whenever I want to have a good laugh about how we, as a species, get along with one another I go to a farm or a zoo. Ever seen a barnyard brawl amongst a herd of cows? Spots vs. Browns? Ever see a bunch of pigs gang up on a lone pig in a pen, really rubbing its face in shit and delivering repeated rounds of kidney shots? Ever seen a chicken lose it on another chicken? How many animals at the zoo hit their kids? Could you imagine the expression on everybody's face if a polar bear started humping its offspring? Sure animals do crazy shit to their own in extreme circumstances, but with humans it's an everyday occurrence.

Animals get the fact that shit works best if you play it cool. Animals reject their own when an individual is deemed a threat to the majority's survival. And if the rejected individual is able to, it simply moves on and seeks out its own place.

Much simpler groups of people have tried to emulate the harmony seen in nature, but the goal is to evolve, not just live in harmony as a means of getting by. And the point of evolving is to improve the quality of life and the experiences had in it. There is nothing wrong with the simple way, save for we are not simple organisms.

Now, because we have evolved to a point where just getting by isn't a problem, we have a lot of freed-up time for our emotions to come into play. Why? Because now we have to fear and hate something other than predators and starvation. Now we can focus our emotions on ourselves and others; the new predators and famines, psychologically speaking. To understand this better we must look at the one thing often mistaken as an emotion – love.

LOVE

Love is a special affection or liking for something. Some people "love" shopping, let's say. But love usually relates to a personal relationship or relationships. You may love your dog, your girlfriend, your friends, your family, or your spouse. So love is basically a strong connection, respect, and pleasurable association with someone, and usually the experience or experiences you have with that person. But that's it. Love is completely devoid of emotion. Love may stimulate emotional feelings, but that's a side effect.

Most people think of "falling in love" with someone as the ultimate form of love. It's not. It's a biological function that makes people bang 24/7 for three to six months in order to have a kid. But, if you're lucky, when the "love buzz" wears off you will still deeply care for and enjoy the company of that person, i.e., you will love them, faults and all. You love your parents, but you don't want to fuck them, right?

Love is the most essential part of a human because it is what enables a person to be a part of another human's life; to add to the experiences of others so that others can add to their experiences and lives. Love is what makes us be nice to ourselves and others. It's the caring glue that bonds people into families, friendships, and societies. Love is all about pleasantry and there's no such thing as tough love, just tough socialization or treatment. Love is that really deep feeling within an experience that opens your eyes to your true innate positive will and desire, and which makes you realize that the same will and desire exists in others.

We all want love. Without it we become the opposite of it. Where there is no love there is a personal and social dissolvent present. We all want to be cared for, to be accepted, and to feel like we're important – a somebody; you may laugh, but it's true. We all want fairness, understanding, and a chance. And whether you know it or not, we all want these things for others and we want to help others realize this by loving them too.

How we go about giving and getting love is another story. People often misconstrue love with attention and ego safety-blanketing. A mind deprived of love can seek it out in odd, often hurtful ways or seeks to hurt others 1) in an attempt to make others feel their pain, or 2) because they lose all compassion and regard for humanity... because they feel people deprived them of compassion and humanity... love.

THE COLLECTIVE CONSCIOUSNESS

The collective consciousness is basically our social contract. It's the rules and accepted beliefs that we're taught when we're young in order to fit in. It helps us survive as a species. It varies from culture to culture and is essential for our survival and development, but for the sake of time we'll stick with the Western one as a guide.

Right and wrong are the two main concepts of our collective consciousness. It's wrong to hurt others, wrong to steal, wrong to be naked, wrong to be jobless, wrong to hit girls, wrong to be fat, and so on. And it's right to be nice to people, to look hot, to have a career, to conform, and so on.

By having agreed upon boundaries in life we can generally coexist more peacefully and productively. And when we all kind of think alike on a wide range of subjects we develop a stronger bond with one another and we become like a herd. Problem is, when you're in a herd, standing out for the wrong reasons means you are wanted out. And so our herd's problem with love begins and is revealed.

The ideas that form our collective consciousness are just ideas, but the people in this, our collective consciousness, may or may not be able to live up to some or many of these ideas. And these ideas that form our way of thinking and actions were created by only a few people throughout the course of our history; usually by people with power over us.

Most people run into problems in life when they fail to meet up to the ideals of the collective consciousness:

-If you're born into a poor family or a broken home.
-If you're of a visible minority.
-If you're not as smart as the other kids who excel in one method of learning.
-If you are physically different in appearance.
-If you aren't cool, and on and on.

Basically, if you can't meet up to the "right expectations" in society or those of your family and friends (which they got from society) you begin to feel less loved, your self-esteem lowers, the hardships of life are felt.

Our collective consciousness allows us to make judgments on people for who they are and what they have done – NOT for the fact that they are a human and can feel and think the same as anyone else in the collective consciousness.

The collective consciousness is a great guide for what to strive for in life, but when it's a guide that passes ill judgment on people because of herd/flock like "norms" based on the whim of the people who made them, we have a problem. And, as such, we must fix it by altering our collective consciousness; expanding it and understanding how our **nature and environment** shape our ideals and behavior.

MIND & PERSONALITY OF THE INDIVIDUAL

To help us further understand what we are and why we do what we do, we need to get a 101 background on what controls it all. If we can get a better understanding of our minds and the brain, and how they work, we can then understand why we do what we do, take stronger control of our minds and actions, and then try to live better lives.

CONSCIOUSNESS:

The thoughts and parts of your mind, psychological components be they emotions, desires, and so on, that you are aware of in daily life. That, and your awareness of the world around you.

SUBCONSCIOUS:

The thoughts and parts of your mind, psychological components be they emotions, desires, and so on, that you are not aware of in daily life, but that may influence your consciousness unbeknownst to you. Many people could live better lives and understand their thoughts and actions more clearly, thereby expanding their consciousness, by coming to know and analysing the content of their subconscious.

PERSONA:

Psychologically speaking, we all wear masks. We all have a variety of our very own personalities we use depending on what situation or what people we are encountered with in life.

When you're with your friends you have the easy/fun mask on. When you're in front of authority you throw on the serious mask. When you're around the elderly you might go for the angel mask. When you are in solitude you wear your less impressive mask. There are as many masks to wear as there are personalities and feelings attributed to those personalities.

The mask we wear the most becomes our character.

These masks are not our true essence; they are the constructs of our ego to help us adjust and function with our thoughts, experiences and society. They are illusionary. Your true essence is conscious energy. Your brain software develops masks to adapt to the surrounding physical environment.

ID:

The part of your mind that urges you to do things. The driving force in the mind. It's the kid that wants everything.

SUPEREGO:

The part of the mind that referees the ID. It's your conscience. It's like a parent, reminding you what's good and what's wrong.

EGO:

An ego is a person's sense of self. It is what you think you are and shapes your perception of your surroundings. The best way I can sum it up is that your ego is the thing that makes you be what you want others to see you as. It motivates you to do things worthy of praise or self-gratification and steers you away from the opposite.

It is the part of your consciousness that identifies you with your physical body, your looks, the sound of your voice, your senses, and other things around you. It makes you see yourself as you, separate from others, and not just a letter jumbled together among other letters. It is an illusion of the mind to help the mind give meaning and purpose to physical existence. When you die so, too, does your ego.

Because your ego is the seat of yourself, your mind, feelings, and the way you want others to perceive you, it is also the thing that causes all of us a great deal of harm. When people feel hurt or threatened, it is the ego that makes us lash out either physically or verbally; if not one of those, the ego becomes overwhelmed and tries to hide problems or, worse, it avoids normal thinking at all just to avoid the pain it suffers from its perception of being hurt.

Now, people with a healthy ego can take hardships in life like insults, beatings, tragedy, disappointment, embarrassment and stuff like that in a relatively good stride. Because they usually have good defense mechanisms, they look for humor in things or they deal with their issues later on in the day and reason them out.

If you know why things happen to you that you don't like, you need to understand the root causes of them in the first place; well-adjusted people know these root causes. They don't get mad when they're yelled at because they assume the dick screaming at them is really just mad about his wife getting stuffed by a guy with more money than him. They don't get mad when someone tries to hit them because they know that people who hit people lack the intellectual capacity to deal with things and must resort to violence as a vent. They can shrug off disappointments with optimism because whatever fell through might not have meant to have been anyways, or they find something else to succeed at, or find an opportunity in failure. And they laugh or make light of their embarrassing predicaments because, hey, comedy is tragedy.

The people who intentionally cause harm to other people's egos are people either defending their ego or trying to make theirs feel better by making yours feel worse. *This is important to know as it's your ego that interprets your animalistic survival mode emotions so intensely and reacts to them in ways that are usually not essential for survival, i.e., stupid, hurtful bullshit.*

THE BRAIN

So it's our egos that drive us towards doing the things that make us feel better about ourselves, to both constructive and destructive ends. But what makes what we do, feel, say, and hear seem so good or bad to our egos? Obviously the collective consciousness and our interpretation of it, but there's more. The same thing that allows the ego to function and exist – the brain. While the ego can affect the chemical makeup of the brain, it's the brain's primal drive that really controls things.

The brain is a big chemical stew full of wiring that transmits these chemicals. The chemicals are what make us feel pleasure and pain, among other things. The brain receives pleasure and pain in two forms: physical and emotional stimuli.

Certain drugs and physical actions can release or trigger the release of chemicals in the brain that give us pleasurable sensations. We all want to feel good so we all do the things that make us feel that way... like eat, drink, smoke, and take the occasional bubble bath while scoring a blowjob. By doing these things our brain rewards us (and itself) by flooding itself with good-vibe chemicals.

Problems arise when the brain becomes addicted to certain physical stimuli (namely drugs, e.g., cocaine) and only rewards us with the good-vibe chemicals on the condition that we consume the drug. The brain can literally become dependent on a physical (in this case chemical) stimulus to deliver pleasure to us. People addicted to drugs aren't bad people. They are people who use drugs for any number of reasons and in the end became dependant on them to feel better than the pain of not being on them.

The human brain, like the brain of a dog, can be trained to obey any number of training regiments; in our case, regimens of socialization and social conditioning. The brain can be trained to adopt certain modes of thought and behavior in exchange for the love, and the pleasure it brings, through social acceptance. The brain can be taught to perceive skin riddled with spots of oil and bacteria as a bad thing. The brain can be taught to perceive large bodies as undesirable. But the brain can also be taught the opposite; people with acne or a few extra pounds could be worshipped by all, if young minds were trained that such things were valuable.

The brain craves pleasure and always opts for the quick fix.* Once the brain has been molded with set patterns of thought and behavior and becomes used to the usual pleasure and security these ways of thought give a person, a person, like the person accustomed to drug-induced pleasure, will rarely seek another means to pleasure and will do anything to maintain its sense of pleasure, i.e., its thoughts and behavior.

If we had fewer restrictions and standards, that are almost always put in place based on the preferences and opinions of a few people in our societies and cultures, then we would allow our brains to gain more pleasure in life by having more options for pleasure available. More options for pleasure in life would make for less of a strain on our egos, the less strain we put on each other, and more room and time for those good-vibe chemicals to swim around.

In the meantime, find out for yourself what ideas you hold to be true that are blocking your path to pleasure in life. As long as no one gets hurt or has something done against their free will, do away with those outdated modes of mind control/training/conditioning and open yourself up to more of whatever you may want or can find.

*When people plan for happiness in the future they are merely coping with the fact that they aren't happy in the present, so they save ego by reassuring themselves with the bullshit that, while they aren't happy in the now, they will one day be happy; it's an illusion, but one that works by tricking your ego and brain out of buckling into immediate depression or anxiousness.

THE SHADOW

There is a place in our minds, our hard drives, where all of the stuff we can't do, say, or be – but that might be a part of us or a true desire - gets stored. All of the stuff deemed inappropriate, even shocking, in our collective consciousness and, in turn, to ourselves... it all gets filed in a place where we don't have to think about it. It's an aspect of the subconscious. It's hidden so well that we eventually forget any of this bad stuff could actually be a part of us... our thoughts, our potentials, our desires. This place or thing that cloaks all that is taboo has been dubbed The Shadow. It is our alter ego, or the exact opposite person we would ever want to see ourselves as.

It's the part of the mind where we hide away any thoughts, character traits, or desires that we feel are undesirable for one reason or another. But there's the catch. Though these things are undesirable they are still a part of you. And until you are fully aware of them and accept them, you will have no real control over them.

The mind is amazing. It forces you to have problems in order to solve them. A person who represses all of their dirty thoughts and habits behind a curtain, so to speak, isn't solving the problem – they're hiding it. So the mind puts these problems back into your life like a series of banana peels on the course of a marathon.

Here is how your Shadow controls you and yet enables you to take control of your unconscious self as well. It starts projecting; taking ideas and qualities you do not like or fear about yourself, and then attributes them to someone or something else, as a means to cope with your shameful/undesirable feelings. You assign the person or thing of your projection with this negative idea and feel safe and comforted because it's not you, yourself, that has this negative aspect to it. But because you're in denial mode, either consciously or subconsciously, you never come to realize that what you have projected is actually your own idea, your idea, just made to look like it belongs to someone or something else.

Through projection The Shadow can reveal, once you learn to spot it correctly, the darker aspects of your personality. By doing so you will start to reconcile with yourself, gain compassion and empathy for others, and will start to truly become and know what it is to be human.

The more carefully you listen to someone who is projecting, the more you start to simply hear them not talking about what they think of someone else, but in fact, what they think of themselves or what they are subconsciously thinking.

Here's an example of projection, the language of The Shadow: I stand up in front of a group of people to deliver a speech and proclaim "You are all dead on the inside. You get up, eat, go to work, and live meaningless lives. Your existence means nothing." That is me taking ideas about myself and spewing them onto people I know nothing about and who may in fact feel quite alive. That is classic projection.

Now here's an example of The Shadow: The homophobe is uncomfortable with the thoughts of balls slapping up against balls that he possesses, because they may be "inappropriate" subconscious desires, so he suspects someone of being a fag, when really he's just uncomfortable with the idea of himself actually taking cork.

And another: The person who rails against drugs only to be busted with a glove compartment full of hillbilly heroin. The person so fears or hates what it is that they desire that they do everything to block out their urges – like yelling and shouting on the radio that people on drugs are scum and should be sent to jail. But because the want for vice and recklessness is demanding to be tended to in the radio blow-hard, well, after a while his anti-drug facade cracks and he gives into that sensual pleasure of doing what's wrong; and medicating any other issues they may have.

And of course: Ever heard of the person who said "I can't believe I did that" or "I would have never of thought they were capable of such a thing" or "what would possess someone to do something like that," in response to brutal actions? Whenever someone commits a despicable crime or act you can be sure The Shadow, and not some devil or evil spirit, was lurking behind the offenders motives. When someone lashes out, the true animal nature of the human spirit comes to light. Remember that the biggest light casts the biggest shadow. And vice versa.

And some more: Even whole groups of people can have a Shadow. Whenever a country gets self-righteous and declares a common enemy, the shadow comes out to control the stage. The projection starts with lines like "The enemy is a brutal, intolerant, and egregious threat to our safety and civility... they will stop at nothing to take from us what is rightfully ours... They are a people who commit atrocities against their own people"... and so on. So you get the leader of a nation, or an influential speaker, churning out a common theme about a common enemy and how this enemy embodies everything that you're not and everything that the country doesn't want to be. And then what does everybody do? They go out and commence a great slaughter with the common enemy and act and become just like the thing they hated so much. In the last two thousand years billions of gallons of blood have been spilt over which group of people were more devoted to a more just God or who were more civilized. More recently, Hitler's main pitch to Germany was that Germans were the only people fit and civilized to rule the world. And then these fit and civilized people went about robbing land and organizing human extermination.

In Russia, Stalin painted Hitler as the bad guy and ended up being worse than Hitler to his own people. Mao got the Chinese geared up over how evil the elite classes were, only to become the worst thing the country had ever dreamed of. And in the early 21st century we had a leader who painted Islamic terrorists as evil for the ways they hate freedom and kill innocent people - only to go on and wage wars that have killed over a million people, and promote laws that infringe upon freedoms.

See how it works? The Shadow is the dark side and it's a part of everyone, not just the bad guys. Realize it, find it, and you'll learn from it how to avoid being and doing what it represents; if being and doing what it represents is harmful.

Once you come face to face with your Shadow, or dark side, you've come one step closer to knowing who you are. You see and feel emotions for what they are; feelings to be controlled and expressed in productive ways. You know your true nature and are freed from any guilt, fear, or shame of it. You become ready to become whole - an individual.

GETTING IN TOUCH WITH YOUR MASCULINE AND FEMININE SIDE

The male and female mind have the exact same potentials. Through socialization different potentials are emphasized and, as such, become dominant forces in the makeup of the mind. The hormones, testosterone and estrogen also push the sexes towards certain mind-sets.

Men are generally predisposed to traits of decisiveness, aggression, and dominance. Women are usually predisposed to traits of compassion, understanding, and nurturing. A well-balanced person possesses all of these traits as a strong suit, regardless of sex. And we are hard-wired to discover and incorporate the ideals of the opposite sex into our personality.

For men, the feminine traits of his personality are represented by the Anima archetype. An archetype is the model or mold of something; the weird word Anima is some ancient Greek or Latin shit. Anyway, for women, the masculine traits of her personality are represented by the Animus archetype. These respective archetypes are the ideal version and example of what each sex sees the other sex as being. The goal is to identify this "ideal version" and realize that it is your idea to own and use as a guide to develop a more complete psychological makeup.

The best way to find your Anima or Animus? When you fall head-over-heels in love with someone. You don't even know them, yet you love everything about them; they can do no wrong. This is an example of your Anima/Animus projecting itself onto the object of your desire. It's not really love (though it may be should you appreciate the person for who they are after the projection fades). It's casting out your idea of the perfect soul mate onto another person.

The ideas and feelings are real; they are what you think a real and perfect man or woman should be. What you need to do is capture these ideas of understanding or decisiveness (whatever you want/like/lack) and realize that they are actually a part of your potential; a part of your consciousness.

Do this and, for a man, you'll learn to be more compassionate, understanding, and loving.

Do this and, for a woman, you'll learn to be more assertive, decisive, and courageous in your life. And because most people are unaware of their projection, once it wears off we see the other person for what they are; not perfect and ideal in every way; rather, we see them as a person with flaws and limitations.

As I like to put it, for a guy the Anima is the white angel that comes to rescue you when you're wounded in battle. She comes to your rescue and takes you to safety where she holds you in her arms up against her titties. She says it's alright, kisses your forehead and heals you; like a nurse, but NOT SEXUAL IN NATURE.

For a chick, the Animus is the dark hero on the horse who comes to her rescue when the town is being pillaged. He throws her up on his horse and slashes his way through the invading forces and onwards towards safety. When they reach the final destination they do not bang.

Now, before the feminists get on my ass, let me say that this is not to say that women are incapable of saving themselves and need a man's help. Quite the contrary; this image serves as a guide for women to realize their own potential and that they should be the guy on the horse and not wait around for one. So, too, for men and the woman in white; men should see that they have the capacity to love, listen, and heal just like any woman can.

Failure to integrate these archetypes into our minds results in cold and oppressive men and weak and dependent women. And if they become dominant in our minds we get weak and dependent men and cold and oppressive women.

INDIVIDUATION

The point of being a person is to experience the most life has to offer, and to be able to enjoy those experiences the most you can. Some people believe the point of being a person is to submit to the will and laws of some God or a collective ideology. Me, I like my idea more... and it's more reasonable too.

The point of individuation is to discover the different aspects of our minds, understand and integrate them into our personality, and see yourself as a person separated from a collective group of people. This process and knowledge enables a person to embrace their true nature and calling in life; what they can contribute to themselves and others; whether through their work, hobbies, family or social life.

And as a bonus offer, when you become fully conscious of your personas, your ego, what is subconscious and conscious in your thoughts/desires/dislikes/potentials and so on, you discover what it is to be human and take the first step towards knowing the human condition; because our minds all follow the same constructs.

By knowing the human condition you can relate to others because you are in tune with how your mind works and can better relate to and understand what other people feel and think and why they might feel and think the way they do.

Failure to individuate can result in a meaningless life and physical and/or psychological illness.

IDEAS

They're the things we use to store and convey information. They come from individuals and gain acceptance from being proven correct, being agreed upon as socially acceptable, or by being forced on people by authoritarian force. Ideas can advance people's lives or hurt them. Ideas can be proven or they can be beliefs. The only ideas I have any belief in are the ones that can be proven or reasoned with.

Ideas can open your thoughts and opportunities to more experiences in life, or they can shut the door. Be careful as to what ideas you hold to be true.

The worst ideas are new ones. Not because they are inherently dangerous, but because they are something we may not understand at first and which can threaten the current ideas and beliefs that comfort us. Groups of people are dumb because they usually take years to several decades to adopt new and better ideas; ideas that eventually help people.

Be open-minded. Question things and think for yourself, but don't worry about conventionalism and what your friends or people on TV think is normal. Normal is just an idea.

WHAT IS THE PURPOSE TO LIFE?

There isn't one. Kind of cold, but it's true. Every purpose you can think of is usually just an idea that someone came up with to fill a void. Every species exists as part of the ecological system on this planet. Animals and life with minimal consciousness are part of a food chain; they grow, eat, reproduce, die, and their reproductions repeat the process into perpetuity, barring prohibitive ecological changes. Our purpose, if you will, is the same, but we have the ability to have a much broader, more intense, range of experiences.

Since the birth of our species it has been our innate desire to seek out comfort from the obstacles we face in life; in this vein we can assume that work (obtaining food/shelter/snatch) is a requirement for living and an obstacle; procuring it leads to satisfaction, i.e., a positive experience. It's almost more of our function in life, than our purpose.

Any purpose given to life is a subjective idea. You can assign any purpose to life; though many are better than others. Right now our purpose is to have good jobs and affordable things, i.e., security, materialism, to prosper in a free land... blah, blah, blah.

What about this one? The purpose to life is to have as much fun as you can, at no one's expense. To exist with as little effort as possible, but to be able to work at what inspires you as much as you want. To make a difference in your life and, if the difference is welcomed, in other people's lives. To make life as a human a better experience today. To be educated and have opportunities. To be happy. To be free. To have the want to help others and be in an environment where others want to help you; to truly feel a bond with humanity. To know what we are, where we came from, and where we are going. To experience altered states of consciousness. To do all this shit and still pay the bills.

The point is - we're all going to die. What counts is the good memories you had before you do.

CAN WE MAKE OUR OWN PURPOSE TO LIFE?

Yup. Because we can. So long as it's open to change when change could improve on something, sure, why not?

FREE WILL

We're in the 2000's and there still isn't a solid definition. Free will is a person's ability to express their wants, needs, and desires. When a person cannot think, act, or say what they wish, their free will is being restrained or curtailed. A person's free will should only be restrained or curtailed if their will is explicitly intent on harming another person or sentient being (see New Moral).

A person's free will should only be curtailed if they HAVE harmed another person, or have demonstrated or expressed the will to do so.

Why is free will such an important concept and why must an environment that allows people to exhibit their free will exist? Because free will is essential for experience. We are here to have an experience. Without free will in the mix we, as individuals, are not in control of our lives, our choices, and our experiences; our reason for being here. Free will facilitates the purpose of life.

Obstructing free will where the will has done no physical harm, or no intended psychological harm, is the essence of evil.

LIFE IS LIKE A DREAM

It is. Like a dream, life can be pleasurable and desires can come true. And also like a dream, life can be depressing and terrifying. A dream, like life, has a beginning and an end. But the advantage life has over the dream is that we have more control over our actions in life.

Life could be, and it is but most of us don't see it so yet, a virtual dream; our dreamscape where we could turn our fantasies and pleasurable dreams into realities. A life without dreams is useless. A dream without a life/reality to live it out in is useless.

THE WILL TO POWER

All people want power. Sure we want sex, but power gets you money and money can buy women, for you and your friends. With power you can obtain more of what you want. Power is the ultimate ego boost. Remember how your ego is the way you want others to perceive you? Well, with power you put yourself in a position to be perceived as anything you want.

Being in power is being in control over something, someone, or people; the only thing you should want power or control over is yourself. But it's the people with the least power over themselves who seek out power over others. When you have power or control, people usually have to answer and look up to you. This makes most people with the power feel good about themselves, makes them even feel superior to others.

Be extremely wary of people who seek out any kind of an authoritative position. People who seek out power are usually lacking in self-confidence and love; they've either received little of it or learned of it in warped ways – or they gain feelings of self-confidence and love through the submission of others. That, or they just plain old want the trappings that power can afford them.

Every time you see someone power tripping you are witnessing a person raising their self-esteem and self-perception of being more important than others (because they don't have any, and aren't) at the expense of the person or people they are tripping on, by making that person, or those people, feel less important. Most importantly, a person in power can impose their ideas (usually tainted by tainted experiences and personality traits) on other people.

Instead of a will to power over people and things, we need a will to power over the self, the individual.

THE NEW MORAL

A new guide, not a law or a command, just a guide to help everyone get along. Here it is... There is nothing wrong with whatever a person says or does as long as it does not, or is not intended to, hurt someone or a living sentient being physically or psychologically, or prevents someone from expressing or exerting their free will. Basically, what's wrong with what you do if no one gets hurt?

If a person does or says something that you deem offensive, it's just an assault on your ego and its preconceived, subjective notions of right and wrong. If someone does get hurt and it was an accident among consenting people acting on their own free will... accidents, like life, happen. What is wrong is making someone feel wrong when they haven't done a thing to hurt another person or forcing them to do something they don't want to do.

We have the ability to make and adapt to new, more relevant laws; laws that are more in accordance with human nature and, as a result, less conflicting with our desires and nature.

ONLY GOD CAN MAKE LAWS?

We are God in that we are of part of God. God doesn't do anything for us. Can you consult and debate with this... "God"? We're here on a floating rock and it's us, and not a "God," that grows food, builds homes and educates one another.

When there is a fire, it's people that come to the rescue, not "God." When your heart stops pumping, it's people that get it going again, not "God." Any law or moral ever made was man-made.

We have the ability to make and adapt to new, more relevant laws; laws that are more in accordance with human nature and, as a result, less conflicting with our desires and nature.

RELIGION

If you have no time for this shit, skip to pg. 51. Otherwise, back in the day it served two purposes. One, as an explanation to and for the mystery of life. The other, being an aggregated combo of social reform and justice. People would have always given reverence to some form of God out of superstition and hope, but then came shamans. The shaman was a tribe's spiritual healer, guide, and moral bastion. As people had more of a means to spread news of things, i.e., common languages, what were once shamans came to be known as divine incarnations and prophets; like the likes of Anu, Ra, Chaos, Abraham, Jesus, Krishna, Mohammed and many others that never had the same following.

These incarnations and prophets all share many things in common, but most importantly is that they all had their own ideas to share with people. Ideas that were aimed at helping people get along with other people and themselves in the hope of living better lives and getting to a better place when they died. And like anyone who is a convincing communicator, offering a message of hope, well, people listen and start to follow; especially when that person claims that they were instructed by a higher power, or, even better, that they are divine.

But of course people die; even the messengers of "God" and even the people who claim to be "it," or an integral part of "it." And when they die they usually have a pretty big following, or some determined friends and beneficiaries who want to spread the teachings. But unfortunately these teachings are lost on most of the people left behind because they aren't even close to enlightenment, i.e., seeing reality for what it is.

And so the faithful spread the word and works of these men until cults are formed; if they didn't exist already. Sometimes people could choose to join and other times they are forced to with threats against their reputation, property, or lives.

And as these cults grew in number, or by years in existence, they became more organized and gained legitimacy as religions. And when you have organizations, you get religious leaders and people willing to comply with the demands of these leaders if they believe it will keep them in the good books with the God the leaders are representing.

That's how and why the earliest forms of Government were actually run by religions, and why it's such a big deal if you live in a land that separates the church from state. Why? Because in a land run by a state, the people can decide to live by their own rules based on, by and large, reason and democratic input, and not the laws and teachings imparted to an individual who lived centuries earlier; left open to the capricious interpretation of a few individuals who then pick and choose parts of these "laws and teachings" (that almost always infringe on free will) and administer them as a guidebook for everyone to live by.

Governments must be absolutely free from organized religion because we are citizens of a country who can vote on how we live. We're not citizens of a religion who must obey the doctrine and moral guidelines of a belief system that we cannot control, i.e., **Religion is not democratic**.

So in a nutshell, religion is an organized attempt to bring people into harmony with each other and a particular God. But it doesn't work, like any imposed system.

Most, if not every religion discourages or forbids questioning or challenging its tenets and dogmas (rules and beliefs). And this is limiting because when you close the door to open debate,* no matter how seemingly true or untrue something is, well, you close the door to the chance for new opportunities that can lead to things people never knew about; namely, progress. Religion requires you to give up your free will. *This is why free speech is crucial.

All religions are cults. Some bigger, some smaller; some more accepted through their long-running history, some less accepted because of their short history. They have concepts that you must believe in order to be a member of the group; they collect money in the form of taxes or donations, they warrant threats to people if they stray from or do not abide by their dogmas in the form of excommunications/expulsions, they have prescribed ways for "moral" living, they usually rely on proselytizing (converting) people who believe in something else to join the group (especially unsuspecting and approval-seeking children), and they view their group as the only true way to achieve the means of union with yourself, others, God, an objective - you name it.

Religion is culpable for the justification of, and waging of, war, the destruction of intellectual property, the killing of people for their non-violent acts, the torture and killing of people for their beliefs and ideas, stealing peoples assets and wealth through taxation without representation, causing harm to the way people see themselves and others in light of standards which dictate ideal physical appearances and sexual desires, promoting the execution of people who commit non-violent acts that are not in accord with religious laws, promoting execution, overpopulating and spreading disease throughout this planet by consistently prohibiting practitioners from using contraceptives, giving us the slave-like mentality that we have to labor for five days with only two off in exchange, and doing all of this for and in the name of the thing that made us.

Pretty fucking twisted, if you ask me. This shit smacks of the design of men and not a God, because it is the design of men.

While religion has caused a lot of heartache for people and insidiously limits people's brainpower by structuring their minds, lives, and societies around the teaching of these religions it has advanced us in a few important ways; like these:

The idea that it is wrong to kill people and that you should help out less fortunate people. However, these are notions that are contradicted repeatedly within the same religious manifestos which state as much, and are contradicted repeatedly in the expressed thoughts and actions by many of the practitioners of these religions. And they are also notions that existed before religions; religions merely enforced them.

But of course all religions and their rules always come into conflict with human instinct because religions and people alike lack the full depth of understanding into basic human instinct and psychology. Rules and ideas that were formed centuries ago by men in discord with the facts about what is really right and wrong have persisted to wreak havoc on humanity because people's innate needs and desires are not suited to follow these rules. These rules are largely based on the opinions and idealizations of the men who made them; or the men who had them recited to them by voices or visions – the kind of people we now deem psychotic; and rightfully so.

Religion has failed to bring us into harmony with one another because it has failed to recognize that there is nothing wrong with anything a person does or says, as long as what they do or say does not hurt, or is not intended to hurt another person.

And religion has failed to bring us into harmony with God because it has failed to recognize that we are, by means of energy and consciousness, an actual physical and mental part of God. We are energy manifest into matter that has the ability to take thought and put it into action and/or physical reality. We can rely on each other to bring our hopes and desires through to fruition without faith, but through knowledge in ourselves and our potential and acting accordingly.

Organized religion is now obsolete to the modern person of reason. The Gods of any religion that ever were are merely human projections of human temperament, desire and potentials. Those who believe in religion suffer from delusions and the restraints of ideas that prevent their minds from exploring and doing more. Religion encourages people to place their fate, achievements, and failures in the hands of an imaginary entity – instead of their own. We see religion's power to delude every time an athlete or actor wins something big. What does that athlete or actor say about their God when they lose? Religion prevents people from realizing they are their very own personal savior (the only one who can save themselves) and, instead, leads people to think that salvation comes from outside and external forces.

Save yourself.

RELIGION VS. SCIENCE

Ever heard the joke about the guy standing on the top of the hill during a flood, waiting for God to save him? The day before the flood when everyone hears the forecast, a bunch of people in a truck drive by the man and offer him a ride to safety, but he refuses proclaiming, "God will save me." The next day as the water rises even more, some people in a boat cruise by and offer him a lift to safety, but he refuses proclaiming, "God will save me." And then when the water is at the man's knees the following day a helicopter hovers over him and the pilot instructs him to get in, but once again he refuses proclaiming the same God mumbo jumbo.

And so when the man drowns he gets to heaven and asks God, "What the fuck man, why didn't you save me... I really had faith in you." God laughs and replies "I should have tied your mother's tubes in a chain knot. I sent you a forecast, a truck, a boat and even a helicopter. But, no, you wanted some OTHER kind of miracle you ungrateful, blind dipshit. No, you wanted angels or divine intervention and all the trappings of an artist's or child's imagination. You were too ignorant to see that I gave humans the tool of the mind to be able to do anything a God can do, or anything you think I can do."

There are many angles to the religion versus science debate. Science is a tool that can verify things and with those verifications, knowledge and the ability to create or "do" things results. But the most significant thing science provides us with is understanding through knowledge.

The more we learn about ourselves and the world, the more we learn how to make things work better. And since everything is a part of God, by means of energy – science is an observation of God.

What is done with these observations is open to interpretation. However, if whatever science does, does not hurt a person in the process, there can be no harm; harm to ego perhaps, but no harm in reality.

WHO WAS JESUS CHRIST?

He gets a lot of press. That and the fundamental moral and social traditions, as well as social conditioning all revolve around broken telephone accounts of his life (the Second Testament was written roughly 45-140 years after Jesus died and was continually vetted centuries thereafter). But who was he? Well his name wasn't even Jesus because the letter "J" was not around when the guy we know as Jesus was born (but for simplicity's sake will stick with the J).

Ask people who they think he is and it's either the son of God or God himself, and sometimes both. Catholics and all of the Christian spin-offs see him as the Messiah. But the Messiah is a Jewish concept. And if people of the Jewish religion don't recognize him as such, then is he? No. The reasons that Jews rejected Jesus as the Messiah are pretty cut and dry, yet no one seriously bothers to question why anyone brought the guy into doubt, or wanted him dead. Why did those Jews push for the death of one of their own kind? Because their culture kind of dictated they had to... he was a blasphemer.

Here's the Coles Notes version of things: The Messiah, or Moshiach, is the guy who people of the Jewish faith were promised/instructed to believe would come to them and do the following, ALL IN HIS LIFETIME ON EARTH:

1. Put an end to war. But Jesus didn't and now we can put an end to civilization in less than an hour.

2. Be 100% human. He was, but a council held it to a vote and liked the sound of a half man, half God redeemer; it also jived well with many myths, that depicted virgin births, from centuries before his birth and the notion of a virgin birth could woo people more. So, officially, he wasn't. I can't even believe this is a debate.

3. Disseminate the knowledge of the one true God throughout the world. He didn't. Today people worship a Santa Claus with horns and there are too many religions and sects within them to count.

4. Help out Jewish people by returning them from exile and rebuilding a temple. No, not any of those either.

5. End physical sickness and hunger. Cancer and food banks, anyone? The catch is that he'll take care of all the unfinished business when he returns, but that's not in the Jewish contract and, as such, he isn't the real deal. Jews

were aware of this in his day and that's why they had to do away with, what they and their books considered to be, a false Messiah.

The fact that Jesus died before helping bring peace to the earth, and Jews, proves that he wasn't the savior promised to the Jews, i.e., the Moshiach. For over 2,000 years Christians have denied and been unable to get this. Me, I think it's all comical, save for the execution part.

~

But the miracles! What for the miracles? He didn't perform any. But just as there are people who believe that an obese senior citizen slides down chimneys with a sac full of toys once a year, there are people who believe stories in a book, word for word. Let's briefly examine the big miracles and see what they represented.

MYTH: Pulling fish and loaves of bread out of a basket like rabbits at a magic show. **REALITY:** His message to the people quenched their hunger for truth and hope – it satisfied them.

MYTH: He cured a person suffering from leprosy. **REALITY:** He wasn't afraid to touch or comfort the sick.

MYTH: He brought a dead guy back to life. **REALITY:** He showed hope to a guy who was gravely depressed.

MYTH: He made a blind guy see. **REALITY:** His words changed an ignorant guy's outlook in life.

MYTH: Instead of swimming to a boat, he walked. **REALITY:** Water is a symbol of emotion; usually difficult and unfamiliar emotions. With such strong character and resolve, problems that would drown most people were a cakewalk for Jesus.

MYTH: He turned water into wine. **REALITY:** Prohibition sucks. He probably showed up to the wedding with booze and let people feel alright with indulging.

MYTH: He rose from the dead. **REALITY:** He didn't come back to life, walking around with holes in his hands and feet. We all rise when we die.

Our energy changes states and one day we may all very well end up being energy that comprises a human once again.

~

I like his main lessons like, for instance, forgiveness and letting people know that judging people is wrong because no one is perfect – but if only he didn't contradict himself by promising to come back and judge people and send those he can't forgive for their sins to an eternal fire; the same motif played out in many myths before and even after his time.

I can't believe in the guy because according to Sunday school he wasn't even human, just part human. How can I try and lead my life like Jesus when I'm at the disadvantage of being a lesser being than him? He's some kind of alien if he wasn't even conceived by human sperm.

Every time a person goes through the suffering of pain or death where is this Jesus, or any other figure of a world religion to offer relief? They're nowhere, because they're all, just like Jesus, d.e.a.d. – dead. But for those people who are lucky enough to get help when they are suffering, they are saved by something... people; mere mortals, I know, but they help get the job done just the same.

So who was Jesus Christ? Humanity's only hope? He was just another guy who stirred the pot and got knocked off as a result. A more cynical summary would read out much like a modern societal tragedy: a virgin is impregnated out of wedlock. The father abandons her and his responsibilities. The young mother brings her child into the world in a state of impoverishment, with few personal resources or skills to further herself. Child lacks ability to conform to social norms. Child is convicted of a crime, sentenced and dies by state execution.

HEAVEN, HELL & PURGATORY

None of them matter. They are all delusional realities. Ever been to one of those places? Do you know anyone who has? My case exactly. Folks, when you die, your ego and its perception of reality, as well as your body, all die. You do not travel up to paradise with Aunt Jennie and Grandpa Joe. You do not go to hell with all the pedophiles and murderers. Nor do you go to a place where you work off all off your sins in order to get into heaven. These beliefs are the grand delusions and symptoms of a psychosis; both of which the prophets of the great religions suffered from and were unable to distinguish from when trying to relate their revelations into useful teachings for their reality-bound followers.

When you die your energy is freed from your body and it returns to the source – the mass of energy that is the universe and God. Maybe your energy is at a positive vibration or a negative one when you die, but that's all; you're energy and no longer a human being. It's only a matter of time before your energy is used in the creation or sustenance of something else.

Listen closely. What is true is that earth is a purgatory of sorts. Life can be like the idea of a heaven when the times are good and like the idea of a hell when the times are bad. And the constant up and downs of life make living here kind of like a purgatory – not quite heaven, not quite hell.

Instead of spending any time or attention on imaginary worlds do everything a favor and focus on this one.

JUST A THOUGHT

While the God vs. Devil notion is just a projection of our psyche, I can't help but wonder that if there was a Devil, who had full reign over our world... wouldn't it dupe us by pretending to be the good guy?

Wouldn't it possess people's minds and tell them to instruct others to follow its laws?

Wouldn't it devise these laws to conflict with human instinct, desire, and nature so as to embroil humans in perpetual conflict?

Wouldn't it divide people in their beliefs and language in order to create conflict?

Wouldn't it group the population into cultures with separate rulebooks that all had the story of their fate end in destruction for many, but salvation for those who abided by the flawed rules of only one book?

Wouldn't it want people to not focus on the pleasure they could have in this life, but, instead, focus on the pleasure they could have in another imaginary one?

Just a thought.

THE END OF THE WORLD

The same drive that pushes us towards creation and accomplishment, which gives us the perseverance and tenacity to overcome obstacles... can be used to destructive ends.

The death drive can be healthy if something is destroyed to be replaced with something better. But it usually manifests in people when they feel despair towards things out of their control, or when they realize they have no control over their own affairs. The death drive, or a wish for destruction, lurches in all our potentials.

The death drive, be it a person wishing for the end of the world, detesting humanity, or wanting to end their life, can only exist in the presence of perceived loss. Hatred is a feeling that can only follow happiness. A person cannot condemn something as bad unless they've had a previous good experience in which to contrast it against.

A person who hopes for the end of the world, hopes so only because they lack something positive that the world once gave them; and they usually project their shortcomings and feelings of ineptness onto what they see as someone else's shortcomings. Because they no longer have the positive thing(s) the world once gave them, they want the world to feel their pain – they want it to end. People and groups with this mindset fail to realize the world will end. It ends for us all the moment we die. Why rush everyone else's death? These people fail to realize that you can, and should, only be concerned with your own personal affairs, unless someone else is directly affecting them in an adverse way.

The death drive is best exemplified in religions. While everything has a beginning and an end, focusing on a grueling and bloody conclusion to life as we know it is nothing short of a psychotic death wish. Sadly, the apocalyptic death wish scenario of the world ending in catastrophe is a scenario that many people actually contemplate, if not hope for.

Our way of life is bound to end some day (the sun's warmth is finite) but even if there was a nuclear war, some people would survive and the show would go on. And it's not a good thing, as all that would happen is the survivors would carry on and procreate to try and get back to our current state of advancement.

Ending this show would only delay the inevitable – the development of a highly evolved and technologically enlightened species. It's time to remove all of these crazy thoughts of finality and replace them with ideas of moving forward.

If the Mayans were so sage, why didn't they predict their demise? If the prophets were so prescient, why didn't they predict the space travel, condoms, video games, surgery or powdered eggs? Why the fuck are people still heeding the prophecies of people who didn't have running water?

People always fail to realize that things in life will constantly wax and wane. And when they wane, it is our death drive that leads the way to the creation of a new wax, not the end of the world.

A NEW RELIGION?

"What can we see today? I think it's obvious from the bit I've talked about here that mythology has a function, that it takes care of this creature man, too early born. It carries us from infancy to maturity, from maturity to our second infancy, and then out to the dark door. You know how most of the mythologies have told us Daddy and Mother will be out there, the old ancestors, Daddy God, Mother Goddess: you'll enjoy it, all your old friends, go on, don't be afraid to die. It's a sort of psychological nursery school.

There's an image that came to me long, long ago: the other animal that's born too early is the marsupial – the baby kangaroo or wallaby or opossum. These are not placentals; they can't stay in the mother's womb long enough to grow up. So, born at the gestational age of about eighteen days, they crawl up the mother's belly into a little pouch. There they attach themselves to a nipple and remain until they are able to get out and walk.

They are in a second womb, a womb with a view.

I think of mythology as the equivalent organ for man. We need mythology as the marsupial needs the pouch to develop beyond the stage of the incompetent infant to a stage where it can step out of the pouch and say, "Me, voila: I'm it."

Now, in order to aid personal development, mythology does not have to be reasonable, it doesn't have to be rational, it doesn't have to be true; it has to be comfortable, like a pouch."

- Joseph Campbell

Here we have, when he was alive just a short while ago, arguably the greatest authority on the subject of mythology in the world. A few pages after this quote the man goes on to say that religion is mythology misunderstood. I love how he dismisses religion with that nursery school line much the same as a grown adult calmly brushes off a bratty child interrupting a conversation (interpretation mine).

Mythology is a series of stories and beliefs that people have used for thousands of years to help them make sense of reality. The mind, or psyche, has needs and it comes into conflict with the harsh realities of life; mythology helps the mind cope with these realities.

Mythology can also reveal to people that the answers to obstacles in life lie within us. The primitive ego has a hard time accepting the fact that it has to destroy another living thing (a buffalo or a cow) in order to survive, so it creates a fairy tale of sorts where the buffalos and cows are spirits and Gods, there to help them and blah, blah, blah; there is a circle of life and no harm, no foul.

The modern ego circumvents this conflict with the convenience that the beef is neatly packaged twenty feet from the personal hygiene aisle, and does away with the need for stories that help us sleep better night after having devoured a living thing.

If you cornered the average person in a secluded room and made them really contemplate where we came from, why we are here, why we have to kill living organisms to live, why we kill each other, why we die young or old or in pain, or where we really go when we die... they wouldn't have a clue; most don't care. The average person who loses a child becomes a mental case. All the questions prefaced with what kind of a God would?... mythology serves to answer this stuff with comforting reassurances; to make sense of it all. To provide some answers and show the way; to help the mind integrate the known and the unknown. To reconcile the outer world with the inner.

The reason why mythology has stuck around, and has been effective for so long, is that mythology was, and is, created by people (not Gods or supernatural beings). It can be related to by people because we all share the same mind - the same software program, our psyches. It is frightening when you look at the similarities between the world's mythologies; the names and places are different, but the characters and roles are all the same. Why? Because we all share this same mental hardware. Every person can relate to the characters who are wise, angry, vengeful, forgiving, understanding, punishing, loving, thieving, fooling, helping, unselfish, selfish, constructive, destructive, peaceful, disruptive, and on and on (remember persona and masks?). It's our mental capacity and potential, all of which is interwoven in the myths of our species which were created by people among our species.

Of course it's all bullshit. But it wasn't to people living thousands of years ago in harsh conditions. It helped them get by. We're more evolved now. We don't rely on rain or migratory patterns to eat. We have homes and apartments with running water and fridges. Sensible people realize that we're all equal and that sex isn't a bad thing, nor is a penis or a vagina. We've outgrown the old mythologies as they are no longer relevant in a modern, technical society. A lot of people, however, have yet to grow up, participating in the traditions of organized institutions that derive their authority and customs from mythology.

He continues...

*"**Now**, what has happened in our modern tradition is that science has disqualified the claims of our major religions. Every cosmological claim of the Bible is refuted; it's a ridiculous image of the universe in contrast with what you see when you peer through a telescope*

in the Mount Wilson Observatory. It's a ridiculous image of history when you look into the abyss of the past opened by archaeologists and palaeontologists. Our whole dependency on this concept of God is not in us but in this holy society has been completely wiped out. No one can honestly say he believes these things; he fakes it: "Well, it's ok, I like to be Christian."

Well, I like to play tennis. But that's not the way we're taught to take it, and so we become disoriented. Add that to the coming in of Oriental, Congolese, Eskimo ideas. We are in a period that Nietzsche called the period of comparisons. There is no longer a cultural horizon within which everybody believes the same thing. In other words, each one of us is thrown out into the forest of adventure with no law; there is no truth that has been presented in such a way that you can accept it.

The whole point of science is that there are no facts, only theories. You don't believe these things; they are working hypotheses that the next bit of information may transform. We're taught not to hang on, but to stay open.

Can the psyche handle it?

There has been one other time in Western civilization when the culture's various myths were at odds in this way. During the last years of the Roman Empire, the Near Eastern religion of Christianity had been imposed on the European individuality. Where the biblical tradition had emphasized the need to subordinate the self to the holy society, the European tradition placed the greatest value on individual inspiration and achievement. During the twelfth century A.D., there was a terrific break between these warring traditions in Europe. It is best represented, if you have a literary bent, in the Arthurian romances, where these knights, parading as Christian heroes, are actually Celtic gods; gods of the Tristan romance, where Tristan and Iseult, like earlier Heloise, said, "My love is my truth, and I will burn in hell for it."

This conflict led, eventually, to the Renaissance and the Reformation and the Age of Reason and all the rest of it. I think where we need to look now is to the same source that the people of the twelfth and thirteenth centuries did when their civilization was foundering: to the poets and artists. These people can look past the broken symbols of the present and begin to forge new working images, images that are transparent to transcendence. Not all poets and artists can do this, of course, because many poets and artists have no interest in mythic themes, and some who have an interest don't know much about them, and some who even know quite a bit about them mistake their own personal life for human life – the anger that's theirs is supposed to be everyman's.

Yet there have been great artists among us who have read the contemporary scene in ways that allow the great elementary ideas to come shining through all the time, portraying and inspiring the personal journey.

Two of the great artists who have guided me in this manner are Thomas Mann and James Joyce. Just take The Magic Mountain and Ulysses. There you have the whole con-

temporary scene – at least as it was around the First World War – interpreted in mythological terms. Well, you'd be more likely to find equivalences of Stephen Dedalus and Hans Castorp than you would to Saint Paul. Saint Paul did this, that, and the other thing, but that was far away in another land millennia ago. We're not riding on horses these days, or wearing sandals – at least, most of us aren't. On the other hand, Stephen and Hans are in the modern culture field. They're having experiences relevant to the conflicts and problems that you're experiencing, and they are consequently models for you to recognize your own experience."

- Joseph Campbell

So, do we need a new religion? No. Religion is mythology that's misunderstood and with a bunch of rules and dogma attached. It's power and control oriented and aims to serve an ideal before the individual. But we could still use some myth to help ground us in the midst of all the chaos that is life. But what myth? Some crazy fool who tells a bunch of fools that he spoke with God when no one else was around? A story of a man being born of a sun, or the son of the sun, or the son of a God - who dies and then is born again, like the cycle of the sun in relation to the sky? All to prove that life is eternal, continuous. Do we need stories that comfort us by stating that even if things go wrong and without justice in our lives, things will eventually be taken care of?

No. There is an alternative.

There is a theme in myths that we could all use in our lives, to add a greater purpose and sense of adventure to our lives – the monomyth: the hero's journey.

We all recognize the hero's journey and love it because it's something our minds are hard-wired to spot and relate to. The person who's bored, trapped in a routine, or not quite sure what to do in life, who then gets thrown into an adventure where they have to overcome several obstacles in order to save the day. They usually make new friends and learn more about themselves along the way.

Star Wars, *The Matrix* and *Pan's Labyrinth* are the best cinematic examples of the hero's journey that come to mind. The more recent book *The Alchemist* is a beautiful story that incorporates the journey. The best artistic works follow the monomyth because it is precisely the story line that we are all looking for and can relate to; it's like water, we all need it and know it when we see it. In real life, the hero can be a woman or a man. We are all heros, waiting to embark on our quest. The different stages of the journey test the hero's and help them to develop their mind's potential; to realize their good and bad traits, to connect with their opposite sex energies and qualities, to face their fears, to experience new ways of life, to seek out and find solutions and to end the journey by giving society something it lacks. And it doesn't have to be society alone – it can be yourself, your family, your work, anything.

Your adventure could begin when you just finish college, you get laid off, you find something that sparks an interest in your life, you experience a tragedy, anything. And you don't have to have just one journey, you can have several of them.

We need a new myth, not a religion. Something we can put to use for the benefit of ourselves and society, and not the "holy societies." A myth that grounds us in this world, but doesn't limit our potential to its boundaries, trends, and norms. Realizing that we must become our own heroes instead of following others and giving them heroic worship and recognition (for the little they ever really do for us), is the new salvation of people. This new way of looking at the trial of life, through the monomyth, could prove to be the next step from nursery school to grade school for our species.

FAMILY

The family has one crucial role – creating new life, protecting it, and fostering it to the point where it can become a self-reliant individual in society. The family is also the refuge of those who run into trouble with life, society, or what have you; the family is the first and most important object of trust for a person.

This is the purpose of marriage; to raise children. But more importantly, marriage is not just a contract between two people to honor and care for each other, but to ensure that they will provide their children with all the love and means necessary to have a normal and healthy life; something grossly overlooked by most parents.

Before you have a kid, you should ask yourself – can I afford the medical costs, clothing, food, daycare, education, dental, books, toys, sports, allowance, and on and on? Most people don't, or go ahead and have children regardless. As a result, we get "society" stepping in to provide for all of the shit needed by the kids produced by a bunch of, by and large, fucking idiots. Remember, life owes you nothing. You have no rights, save for freedom, liberty and access to an attorney to defend them both.

A family doesn't have to have a man and a woman as parents. All of the fucked up people in our history came from heterosexual parents. The only thing that counts is whether the people raising you do so with unconditional love and guidance, and that they have the resources to get your feet on the ground. The family is where kids really learn how to socialize, communicate, and learn – and they do so with the help of their siblings and parents and constantly being around them. The lessons and "rules" instilled from experiences in the family setting are then used in the real world.

The family is one of the greatest influences on the development of the mind. The superego is molded by the morals and values of the family. The instilled love, confidence, security, and teachings, or lack thereof, by the family shapes the ego of a kid. What a family does or doesn't like and what a kid doesn't like or likes about their family can all influence a child's id and subconscious. The family can build a kid's Shadow and can provide the foundation for a kid to relate to their respective anima or animus.

Parent's personalities leave indelible imprints on their kid's personalities, for better or worse. Parents usually project their shortcomings and insecurities onto their children (that they may have learned or developed from their parents) and in time a vicious cycle develops as children pass negative teachings and traits onto their children. Kids are a reflection of their parent's and their parents teaching... keep this in mind at all times. This is not to say that every kid from an unstable home will be a fuck up and that every kid from a stable home will be normal – but a good environment is a good environment; a good start is a good start.

The first thing a child can trust, and is designed to trust, is the family. When the family harms a child in any way, or if the child perceives the family as untrustworthy, the child usually becomes non-refundable, non-exchangeable damaged goods.

I agree with people on the whole that if you need a license to drive a car you should need one to have a kid (not to sound gay), if it were not for the fact that control over your body is a right of free will and not a privilege. Personally, there are too many fools having kids; kids, on an intellectual and even literal level, having kids. How dangerous is it that we have huge segments of the population producing more people who will be raised with poor opportunities, comforts, or training and life skills? Kids being raised by parents who have relationship issues, drug addictions, money problems. What a mess, and I'm just scratching the surface. The only hope is for the kids who come from undesirable families to educate themselves about their problems, better themselves, and do better for their kids.

Every child that is born is given the chance to experience a wild new world. But is that world worth coming into? Will that child be able to live its dreams? A child has to endure a lot of physical and emotional pain growing up; is it worth it for what society has to offer? Conversely, every new child has the potential to offer society a great deal; does society have what it takes to allow that child to deliver on its potential?

This whole business of having kids because "it's what we do" has got to be put on pause for a second. Why? Why have them? I know we're biologically compelled to, but I also know that condoms were invented by popular de mand. Personally, I think you're a fucking idiot for wanting to have to look after someone (the "you'll understand once you have one of your own" novelty wears off after a while) for 18-30 years. I know we have a tradition of having them; is it so that we can validate our reproductive systems or fantasies of being grownup? Are there really that many fucking idiots out there trying to fix relationships with a pregnancy? Most people learn how to change a diaper after their first kid is born, let alone know what their kids' minds and bodies need to develop properly.

I believe the huge volume of children we bring into this world devalues life; easy come, easy go. If life was great for everyone then, sure, pour them out like table waters. My solution is to do what most educated people in the world do: have a kid or two – no laws, social pressure, have more if you want, but just try and keep things manageable; not for the environment's sake, just ours.

We must remember that our families and societies have to be the ideal world for a human with higher consciousness to come into.

The best way to create this ideal platform is through having loving, warm, understanding, and free-thinking families for children to explore and mature into the world from.

Two parents, one parent, five parents, foster parents, stepparents, god-parents, whatever – give them love, confidence, knowledge, and the ability to move through life being able to think for themselves.

WOMEN VS. MEN

No doubt about it - women are inferior to men. Just kidding. Both are equal, save for their respective biological differences. Without the two sexes, sex for most of us wouldn't be as much fun. Given that each sex is predisposed to certain psychological traits (Anima/Animus) both sexes can learn from each other to become more complete.

Women have traditionally been held back in society on account of their relative physical weakness to men, which has prevented them from literally fighting for equality. That and childbearing, coupled with society's expected role for women as the stay-at-home caregiver, have stifled women's ability to assert their talents and desires in the past.

It goes without saying that to deprive women of anything that society has to offer is to deprive half the species of vital potential. Inequality and disparity towards women in work, education, liberty, and respect shines a spotlight on ancient and regressive attitudes.

Gender roles are a product of social behavioral conditioning – the norm, the made-up social contract, our collective consciousness. A man can take care of a baby just as well as a woman if he lets himself and wants to. A woman can run any business just as shrewdly and confidently as a man if she wants to, or learns how to like any man is taught. A man can sew and cook just as well as any woman. A woman can be into sports and drinking beer just like a guy if she is encouraged or exposed to such activity at a young age. A man can make clothing out of animal skin if he has to. A woman can hunt if she must. If there were girls in G.I. JOE ads and boys in Barbie ads, girls would have Cobras on their dressers and boys would have Barbie and Ken dollhouses in their sandboxes.

Your sex is determined by the chance you develop one extra chromosome or not. Your sex is just the body your ego resides in. Our true essence is sexless.

THE LOTTERY OF LIFE

The type of family you're born into, whether it be rich or poor, loving or abusive, encouraging or oppressive, the type of body you're born into, whether it be female or male - healthy or unhealthy, your race... all of the things that predetermine your chances for success in life are out of your hands; this is not to say you can't overcome unfavorable odds, but it's just to say that starting at an advantage is better than a disadvantage and that it's not your fault if you start off in an undesirable circumstance.

Being born into the body of a person that society idealizes is like winning a lottery ticket. If you're born in a First World nation you've won bingo. If you're born into a family that has enough money that money isn't a worry, you've won the lottery. And if you're born into a rich family with the right connections and looks, you've hit the jackpot. But in the lottery of life there are a lot of losers, not really losers, but just people who don't have it that easy from the get go, who have to work that much harder to strive for the top.

Whether you're looking up or looking down... no one is special.

SEX

I can honestly say it's one of the best things in life. There's nothing like trying to convince a woman of your fuckability, and then savoring time with her in her bed, on her dining room table, in her shower, or, sometimes, in a bathroom stall. There are as many kinds of sex as there are kinds of food; passionate, quickies, rough, sensual, slow, make-up, break-up, cheating... all of them natural and healthy as long as they are explicitly consensual.

Sex can take people on an adventure and a process of maturity. For me, the more I banged, the more I learned about life, myself, women, and how to be happy. There is nothing like rushing to work, getting home, or having, if time permits, a nice brunch the day after getting laid with a new broad; it's the best feeling in life. Even if I only have a couple of smokes on me and five bucks in my pocket, I feel like a fucking champ every time I walk out of a new apartment or down an unfamiliar driveway. The times I had a hard time getting the job done, or just couldn't get it up, well, those are some of the best stories.

Have I ever contracted an STD? Of course! Do hockey players ever get their teeth knocked out? Of course! It's all a part of the game. Have I been hurt by women emotionally? Yes, and I'm a stronger person for it on account of having to face the reality of rejection and the illusions and assumptions that desire can create. I've loved kind women and crazy bitches of every stripe; the latter of whom do the silly shit like try and get pregnant, spy on you, spread rumors, hide other relationships, show pictures of your dick in their mouth to their boyfriend, threaten to kill themselves, hide their drug use, try and bait you into hitting them, and the other bullshit that any person doesn't need in their life.

The kind women have shared their homes with me, great concerts, boring movies, awesome meals, wine, road trips, life-enhancing conversations, and the warmth of ineffable human connection; love. As a result of all of this, I have some cool memories and more compassion for people.

But there are a lot of people who are afraid to live life to the fullest. They feel weird about their bodies and sex. Some people think reproductive organs and sex are bad things. Some people even think sexual thoughts and desires are inappropriate. These people are repressed; they aren't free. I'm not saying promiscuity should be a convention, but I am saying that there is nothing wrong with anything sexual in nature. I'm saying, feel free and normal to do what you want with your body. Be smart and go out there and fuck somebody.

RACE

Every person of every race has one thing in common – they're all part of the human species. It's not the human race – it's a species. Different physical traits, features, cultures, and languages are what separate and distinguish the races. What causes problems among the races is when our emotions kick in out of fear for something unknown or different, and when our egos need to assert themselves as stronger and better than others. Also, a lack of understanding and insight into the human condition allows for racial tensions.

Only a fool would believe there are no racial divides remaining in the West, let alone the world. But, only a fool would take a racially-dividing stance or hold a racially-dividing perspective. Luckily, racial divides are narrowing. People of all skin pigmentations are starting to get their deserved stake in life. In time, if it isn't the case already, the white man will be the minority in the world.

If there's one thing I've learned in life here, it's that you can only understand people one at a time. Racism doesn't take this into account. It's why racism is the height of ignorance; though the irony is that it's most often learned ignorance. I'm a big believer that, at least today, racist slurs and insults are just quick and easy ways for people to vent when they're frustrated or need a quick joke; sadly, most people interpret and react to words (or combinations of them) that they don't like, in the same manner most rational people would react to seeing a daycare centre on fire.

The best way to bring the races together is through humor. Comics of every race cracking jokes about every stereotype possible. The more you make light of even the most sensitive things, the less sensitive they become. Humor erodes and dissolves the most oppressive barriers in life. It's why people of oppressed races and cultures are usually the funniest.

Just be careful with how good the joke and delivery is; one time I lobbed one out in a discussion along the lines that crack in the ghettos of L.A. (facilitated and introduced by the C.I.A.) wasn't such a bad thing because the people there had nothing anyways. It didn't go over well.

I guess my point is that after watching a Chris Rock or Russell Peters concert – how can you hold a hateful racial perspective that certain people are inferior to you because of what they were born into and look like?

We're all the same thing, folks; just people of the same thing in different shapes, sizes, and colors. Through time and the mixing of the races (miscegenation) I believe we will one day constitute one race within a single species.

Maybe then the racial race will be won.

ABUSE

Whatever the type, its roots lie buried in the need for control, ego boosts and a lack of compassion and understanding of the human mind. People who abuse others are of every race, income, sex, age, and level of education. All abuse degrades a person's dignity and confidence. There are three common forms: verbal, physical, and sexual. By better understanding why people abuse people we'll be able to better prevent it.

VERBAL: people who constantly criticize, put down, nag, and berate their spouse, kids, or other people usually have negative views of themselves; based on what people think of them and their own failures in life. They take out their frustrations in life on others as a means to distract them from their own issues. The negative critique and comments are never constructive and guidance is never provided; because if the verbal abuser could provide assistance, or really cared, they'd focus on their own lives. Instead, the abuser takes out their inner frustrations in the form of projection and transference.

The abuser, as is the case with any kind of abuse, almost always abuses people they feel less threatened by, or who can be manipulated; family members or people under authority. If the abuser can be made to see themselves for what they are, either by a victim or a person sticking up for the victim, the abuser usually gets really pissed off and retreats.

The only way for the abuse to end is when the victim sees the abuser as having a low self-esteem, doesn't take the abuse personally, and then defends themselves with reason and/or by removing themselves from the situation or environment with the abuser. That can be a tough task for dependent spouses and children, and is the reason why so many people grow up with the scars of verbal (mental) abuse... they lack/lacked the knowledge and ability to avoid it.

PHYSICAL: people who have to hit people do so because they lack communication skills, have weak egos, and use violence to control people. Most victims of physical abuse are hit when they ante up an abuser in an argument, or make their abuser feel volatile or threatened in some way. The violence is used by the abuser to feel in control.

Senseless abuse, like the stereotypical drunk dad at three in the morning scenario, is the product of people who are frustrated with themselves and take it out on others who aren't in a position to oppose them; like so many things in their life do. Sadly, like most abuse, physical abuse is usually learned at a young age. Kids see certain behavior and a lot of them go on to repeat it.

SEXUAL: people who commit rape do so because they can't get laid any other way, for control, for the rush and thrill of a deviant act, and out of spite for the person they are raping or humanity in general. A society that encouraged people to get as much sexual pleasure as possible would be a society with less rape and happier people. It is a proven fact that where porn is poorly accessible, the incidence of rape is higher. As for understanding why people forcibly fuck others for kicks and hate, please see the part about psychopaths and sociopaths.

As for people who sexually abuse (molest) children, the causes are common. Children are easy prey for people who can't get laid. People who are attracted to children to the point where they are compelled to fuck them, against their better conditioned judgment, suffer from a genetic predisposition that is not in accord with society and the overall psychological welfare of developing people. Medication and professional help are used to help overcome people who have these predispositions, but with minimal success; maybe one day these genes may be able to be, voluntarily, altered. There are people who molest children for the sick thrill of it, but this is usually just a part of their reasoning.

A lot of people who molest children were, in fact, molested as children themselves. They pass on the torturous behavior and experiences as a way to reconnect with their forgotten (and stolen) experiences of innocence and because they feel that if it was done to them then someone else should feel what it was like... almost as a way of trying to express and understand their pain and experiences while not wanting to be alone in the process.

As I see it, rape and molestation should be treated just as seriously and punished just as harshly as murder. The victims of these kinds of abuse seldom go on to live normal lives. For those who do cope and move on, they do so with years of work and emotional struggle; often more so than the friends and family members of murder victims.

THE CYCLE OF ABUSE

As should be obvious, it's important to know that most abuse is learned; from seeing abuse inflicted upon others or oneself. What's worse is that most of the people who abuse others don't really want to – they're just confused and frustrated; acting out as a means of temporarily relieving stress and inner conflict.

Even worse, over time, the victims of abuse develop feelings of guilt, inferiority complexes, and the belief that they somehow deserved what they got. It takes a long time for victims to understand that they were just victims of bad circumstances.

WILL IT END?

No. We'll just get better at preventing most of it through awareness, education and getting over it with the same means. Now, if our society didn't have as many peer and work-related pressures, and people were more aware of human psychology, and getting laid was like shaking hands... you'd see abuse in all its forms abate dramatically.

PSYCHOPATHS & SOCIOPATHS

They're people without a conscience, or who don't let it bother them, and who have no remorse for their socially unacceptable behavior. The term sociopath is thrown around so much that psychopaths and sociopaths have become synonymous. They're not. A psychopath is usually less socially adapted and more predisposed to aggression and violence, especially indiscriminate aggression and violence. A sociopath is usually socially skilled and is less inclined to resort to physical aggression and violence.

Your classic psychopath is a person who can kill and rape people of both genders and of all ages, taking pleasure in the act(s), and then go about life the next day cool, calm, and collected. They might worry about getting caught, but they sincerely don't care about the people they've hurt or any morality issues. They have no conscience... the little voice of our ego most of us have had since childhood. A psychopath has that little voice, but it shields the mind from guilt. The psychopath doesn't see people as loving, loved, or worthy of respect. The psychopath sees people much the same as most of us see ants, except with contempt. The psychopath views people as corrupted, unworthy, and as obstacles in their way. They usually fake their emotions through life, as they get little out of it. Their horrendous acts bring, what are for them, "true" feelings of accomplishment, importance, validity and control.

A sociopath has all of the guilt-free, uncompassionate armor of a psychopath, but they use it to achieve, typically, different means. A sociopath can lie, cheat, twist, turn, and manipulate any circumstance or person to obtain what it is they want. Usually having a higher degree of intelligence, they are excellent at climbing ladders in the workplace and managing complex situations and tasks which require boldface lying and deceit to reach a desirable outcome. They are the real two-faces in society; smiling at you one moment, then pitting someone else against you the next to achieve material or emotional gratification.

As for what makes people antisocial to the point where they can do as they please without a care in the world, like most fucked up people, a lot of it has to do with their start in life.

Psychopaths are usually subjected to witnessing or enduring physical and emotional abuse. The pain they feel at a young age, which essentially robs them of the chance to learn real love, desensitizes them to abnormal thoughts and behavior. Psychopaths are usually genetically predisposed to the condition, and the wrong environment merely triggers it off.

Sociopaths are debatably less genetically predisposed to any pathological mental condition. They learn, in time, how to attain things through deceit and immoral behavior. The more skilled the sociopath becomes, the more confident they become in their warped ability to get what they want, and the less remorse they have for their negative actions.

If you want the real difference between psychopaths and sociopaths, it can be seen during the reading of a verdict. The guy who murdered a cop and doesn't bat an eye when sentenced to execution – psychopath. The guy who may or may not breakdown after being sentenced ten years for swindling billions – sociopath. These people aren't crazy. They know right from wrong. They just don't care; they'll go wrong every time if they think it's advantageous.

On a parting thought, while only 1% of the population suffers from these disorders it must be known to all that psychopaths account for 15% - 20% of the prison population and are responsible for 50% of all the violent crimes committed. That's a pretty big impact on the population... it makes you wonder what amount of damage the sociopaths account for in society?

BULLYING

Remember how we've talked about the ego and how it, being you, wants love and on the surface of it all – appreciation, attention, and all the things that make us feel special? Everyone wants to feel socially accepted, loved, and wanted in some form or another. The less love or feelings of acceptance a person has, the more they may try to obtain it with, can I say, effort? And when positive efforts fail to win a person love and acceptance, this rejected person can go about taking matters into his own hands.

Rejection can be a positive thing. It can be used as positive criticism; to be used to guide you towards what you really want and need, or to help you improve yourself by working on what you might lack. But if the rejection is unfounded or oppressive, there are four things people usually do.

A so-called reject can either reject their rejecters and find acceptance among other like-minded people. They can become overwhelmed from feelings of defeat, abandonment and subsequently withdraw from society. They can overcome their rejecters by force. Or, and this is related to the last point, they can retaliate and lash out against them.

By rejecting those who don't like you, won't hire you, won't date you, and so on, you enter the realm of denial – a defense mechanism of the ego; since you don't approve of them, your ego tricks itself, in a useful way, into not being hurt or offended because you "didn't like or need those people/person anyhow" and sometimes your denying these people or "rejecters" is well-founded because they really aren't for you and you'd being doing something more productive with other people.

For those unfortunate people who just always end up feeling like worthless pieces of shit, very sadly they end up giving up on love because it gave up on them a while back. Through a combination of drugs and mental illness they end up disappearing from society by living on our streets, living in self-imposed isolation, and by committing suicide.

For those people who feel rejected or fear the threat of rejection in some important facet of their life, but have the perseverance to acquire love and acceptance at any cost, herein we enter the realm of the bully, the gang, and the tyrant; all three of which are the same thing.

Every bully, while outwardly portraying a sense of confidence and self-esteem, ironically doesn't have much of either; it's a facade. The bully, like some strange kind of parasite, has to resort to making other people feel worse off than themselves in order to feel that they are better than that person or people.

By making someone feel small, the bully feels big; the person being bullied is a virtual stress ball and punching bag for the bully. But it's all an illusion. The bully always goes for the easy target (smaller, timid types that can't physically fend off the bully or who lacks the self-confidence to fend off the bully with reason or by seeking help regardless of threats or peer expectations). While the bully feels like they are smashing through brick walls, they're shadowboxing. Instead of fortifying their ego through an honest sense of accomplishment, their ego becomes founded on something forged through fear; like feeding yourself on empty calories thinking you're full until you die from malnutrition.

The sad thing is that the victim of the bully often feels like there is something wrong with them that justified their being bullied, and they often develop complexes and can even become bullies themselves later in life. And what the bully always fails to realize is that those who do accept them do so not out of true love, friendship, or acceptance, but do so because they fear them, or feel safe that no one can hurt them if they are associated with them.

Society pays a high price for bullying. Bullies, if not thwarted, go on living in manipulative ways, usually unaware of their unhappiness and the suffering it costs others through their actions. And the people who are bullied can be deprived of the confidence needed to live their life to its true potential. If kids and people were taught about the causes and ways in which bullying functioned, instead of simply telling kids it's wrong and punishable, kids would be better able to prevent it through calling bullies for what they are; people who need help, who need to get a life, who need to be cool through getting along with even the people they think are weak or losers.

People who are the recipients of rejection or those who are bullied can often seek revenge on those who reject and/or bully them. Why? Because they feel hurt, they want others to feel their pain... to "know what it's like" and to get even. So in cases where a person or people feel really stepped on, well, their response can be cruel; just like a bully who pushes people down, figuratively or literally, in order to feel better than others.

Common cases of a rejected person lashing out can be seen in the postal scenario; a guy walks into work and opens fire indiscriminately. He's not crazy... just been pushed to the brink. He's in debt, gets no respect where respect is due, his car broke down the other day, knows he might get laid off, the cocksuckers at the bank won't give him a loan, he loves his family and his wife, deep down can't stand the rat race, and his boss yelled at him the previous day for an oversight in a menial chore. So what does the guy do – he feels overwhelmed by the hopelessness of it all. He feels small. He knows he can't do more with his life and he hates the predictable way it's headed. He grows a strong contempt for the job and the people in it that have become his life and then he fucking snaps. Snaps at it all. Snaps at the job, the people he hates who make his job harder, the people who do less and make more, and snaps because he's sad to the bone and feels hopeless; the violence manifested from his unhappiness merely reflects the torture he feels in his life.

When people comment in shock to these stories I always laugh by saying, dude, the guy was pissed off at life, his life sucked to him, he had no help to make it better, do you think he would have killed people if he was taking a great month-long vacation every year and getting a blow job every morning in the shower?

People can snap violently when they've been tortured long enough. Weapons are used because the people seeking revenge are usually not physically imposing enough to deal with their problem hands on, and they want to maximize the pain they can inflict.

The best example of a violent lashing-out is the Columbine incident. There you had two kids who, as a result of bullying, slid into depression and anger, exposed themselves to violent art, and decided that life was pointless for them; and to fuck with the assholes who made their life feel so miserable. And they succeeded in getting their message out and into the collective consciousness through the media; the proof is in how common school shootings have become. I wouldn't justify the Columbine ordeal, but when you're constantly called names, seen as a loser by everyone, and feel like you and life are worth shit, something is bound to give. Doug Stanhope brutally, yet rightly, called the incident what it was – payback.

Kids can be cruel, really cruel. A lot of times kids are bullied by kids because it's socially accepted; kids like making fun of "rejects" in general because it can simply make them laugh, not taking into account the dangerous psychological harm they can cause the person they are teasing. It takes time through maturity for people to learn that you shouldn't get your kicks off at someone else's expense (at least not to their face) and it takes even more so for a wallflower to become cool, or to learn to do their own thing, i.e., party with the people they want to and not with the people everyone wants to. It takes time and experience to individuate – to become you, your own person who doesn't, with sincerity, give a fuck about what other people say or think about you.

Until then, we'll always get artsy kids being called fags and shoved around, shy and fat kids eating lunch by themselves or fearing the mean kids down the hallway. We'll have the kids who want to really learn, getting beats and made fun of for wanting so, and we'll get kids laughed at because of what their parents may or may not do for a living, or where they live. We'll get kids picked on for their clothes and hygiene, and all of that silly superficial shit that many young people are too stupid to realize is stupid; but not so stupid as to not learn the difference if they were taught so.

The best example of bullying in society that I can think of is the bullying that I orchestrated as a child. I always had a problem with my fair share of teachers; some directly and most through my reputation as a kid who did what he wanted, talked back, and distracted other kids. My problems were attributed to ADD, but I was really just bored with the subjects and the way they were taught. I was falling asleep in class as early as grade three. I had a problem with cracking jokes, blowing farts, being the class clown, you know – being a kid. I'd debate with teachers, often making them look stupid and making the class laugh. So in time I grew unpopular with the teachers and never really had their... respect. I couldn't make them laugh, and everything that involved a teacher became an uphill battle for me.

But there was this one kid in, I believe, grade four who was adored by all the teachers. We'll dub him Jimbo. He did what he was told to, had excellent, if not the best, grades, was punctual, never inattentive, pencils always sharp – even the colored ones. He always had gym socks, and the teachers loved talking with him. He wasn't a kiss ass, he was the prodigal student; my antithesis.

The way the biggest bitch (every kid agreed) in the school smiled when she spoke to Jimbo about the minutiae of cooking shepherd's pie drove me fucking nuts. So did I punch the kid out every recess? No. I started a gang aptly named The Hate Jimbo Gang; or it might have been a club or group, I'm not sure, I was eight or nine years old at the time of its inception. I got a group of about six or ten kids to spy on Jimbo, to beat up Jimbo, and maybe even to make fun of Jimbo – anything to bring down Jimbo. And I did so with the incentive of $2 a week to each gang member; the funds stolen from my old man's money jar. I paid the members every Monday with the $2 bills sealed in the school's own stationery, stolen from my mom through her fund-raising supplies.

The funny thing is, nothing ever happened to Jimbo, from what I recall. He never got beat up or spied on, or any of the shit I paid for (through theft). He might have been made fun of, but I think he was already teased before I set out my orders. It was all about me gaining a sense of self-confidence and control at the expense of another person.

The whole thing came down when rumors of a gang spread and the whole trappings of the "organization" were laid out on the table. Everyone involved got suspended for a week, with most of us hanging out, even being taken to a movie by one of my buddy's parents.

Parents and teachers were shocked, horrified, bemused, and almost left with smirks on their faces from the fallout of it all. Who had ever heard of a clandestine gang involving eight and nine year olds, let alone one with a salaried pay structure? It's what can happen when you take a person, regardless of age, make them feel unworthy, offer punishment instead of guidance, criticize them, and ultimately reject them. The whole thing wasn't really about Jimbo; it was the fact that he got the love for being him and I didn't. It brought out the worst in me. In a sick sense, I lashed out against the teachers by trying to hurt the apple of their eye.

GANGS

The things old ladies fear the most. Gangs are really just social units; an organized way in which people get together to form a collective identity. Gangs are social clubs. In the negative light, gangs are the means for people to organize themselves to gain security, status, and money.

Most people join gangs because they don't have much going for them and want to feel important. Gangs are a way for people rejected by the establishment to feel they are a part of one. It's a big ego boost; take a gang member away from the gang and they become the deflated, unconfident individual that they are; but put them in the gang and they feel accepted, powerful, and important. Most gangs derive their power through submitting the will of, and instilling fear in, others. Like any dominant institution, really.

Urban gangs are all about a bunch of young men or women who are powerless in society, but through their gang membership they see themselves as strong people; it's tribal/primitive basics 101. Because they rely on force to assert themselves, and use it at whim, it's always gangs that control the illegal trades like drugs, firearms, and prostitution.

Gangs like bikers are more or less the same, except membership is more about gaining status, as opposed to having nothing to do (or wanting nothing to do) in society. Most people don't realize that most bikers don't make a lot of money being affiliated with biker gangs; it's about the ego.

Although most gang members come from bad homes, it's not a rule of thumb; weak-minded people will always try and find ways to gain power over people in an attempt to feel better about themselves.

But as long as there are illegal commodities and inequities in the opportunities people have to pursue in life, society will always have its gangs.

But there's another type of gang in society. Gangs of the elite. Gangs of people who think they are better than the average Joe, and who think the laws of the land don't apply to them. Using their influence they break and bend rules to get away with nonviolent crimes at the expense of the average Joe. While they don't shoot people down in the street, peddle drugs, shake down small businesses, or make women go down on cab drivers - they do manipulate laws for profit, make people pay too much for essential needs, and make harmful things legal for profit. Most of these gang members come from good homes, have good homes, and know the difference between right and wrong.

At least your traditional gangs admit to being... bad.

DRUGS

If it's your will, use them as you wish. Drugs have been around forever and people have been consuming them just as long. If using them leads you to hurting yourself or others, then you're accountable to the damage accordingly. If your drug use makes you ill and requires treatment then you should pay for it. If your drug use causes harm to another, the same thing should apply, unless, of course, you are forgiven.

No one has the right to tell you what you can put into your body, or to classify you as a criminal for putting something in your body. When Governments outlaw drugs they are outlawing your freedom and your rights; drug use is a personal choice and an extension of a person's free will.

No one has the right to regulate plants that grow in the ground for profit, no one. You should be able to grow any drug (plant) in the world right next to your lilies and hostas. Making drugs illegal creates black markets, criminal activity, and Government corruption. The criminalization of drugs enslaves people who have never hurt other people. If you removed all of the violent and nonviolent drug-related offenders from state and federal correctional facilities... I'm not sure there'd be many people left.

Most people like drugs because they break the redundancy of normal consciousness; drugs alter consciousness. The altered states drugs bring to people can be fun, adventurous, anything really. People who chronically abuse them do so because they're filling a hole in their sense of purpose in life or are avoiding undesirable circumstances and feelings. Should we make not feeling like you have any real meaning in life, or wanting to numb pain, illegal?

Drugs are for anyone to use and for no one to condemn. And they aren't to be regulated and taxed; no Government has the right. Do your Italian neighbors pay the Government taxes on the tomatoes they grow in their backyard?

Folks, it's pretty simple. If you don't like drugs, don't use them. Don't use them and teach your kids not to use them. It's your choice. Don't impose it on other adults.

JUSTICE

Our justice system works, for the most part. It has two major failings; sure there are many, but here are the biggest. One is that people with power and money are not subject to the full extent of our justice system because good lawyers can shield their clients; this isn't a bad thing, it's why lawyers are a good thing. If a celebrity or politician gets pulled over after speeding, under the influence of alcohol, and is found with a bag of cocaine in their lap – they should go to jail just like an electrician or carpenter would. Sounds pretty obvious and sensible, right? Then why is it just not the case? We need equal justice for all. The only solution is for judges to lay down the law with the impartial knowledge and skills they possess.

The other problem with the justice system has to do with what we consider a crime in this country and how we punish people who commit violent crimes.

Jail is the way we punish the bad guys. We remove their free will and remove them from society by putting them in cages and giving them an hour of recess every day. The best part of it is that we call jails correctional facilities, when all they really do is make people more incorrect. I can understand how jail works for nonviolent offenders; you go in and learn a new skill and/or think about things for a long time and feel the punishment. Spending a few years in jail for theft or minor assaults... I get it; sit in the penalty box and don't do it again when you get out.

But for people involved with drugs and serious violence we could save ourselves a lot of time and money* by doing a couple of things. We seriously need to decriminalize the consumption of drugs and the selling and production of drugs. These activities aren't violent and are matters of free will and personal choice. It's just a fact that if people could produce, sell, and consume drugs freely, there wouldn't be many people left in jail.

Does some kid from a poor neighborhood need to spend ten years in a cage for selling a powder that someone was willing to pay him twenty dollars for? How many kids from poor neighborhoods try to sell six-packs on street corners? How does snorting a line of powder in a bathroom to feel alert and talkative make me a criminal? Does drinking a substance that makes me laugh louder, impairs my mental judgment and sometimes makes me aggressive (even though at 175lbs I'd be wise to never get aggressive) make me a criminal?

You either get it or you don't.

Next, for all violent offenders, we need to reintroduce the only moral and sensible form of punishment available. You're going to laugh, but I'm serious. The penal colony; call it New Australia. I'm not kidding. An isolated and monitored island with no chance of escape and no provisions, save for the resources on it; one for the girls, one for the boys.

If you're violent, exempting self-defense, to the extent that you kill someone, or attempt to, you forfeit your right to live in society; not your right to free will, but your right to live freely in society. You are a threat to society and punishing you is a burden to society. But, so as to not infringe on your rights as a human to be free, you, the violent offender, will simply get to live free with other people who have done similar things, i.e., inflicted pain and deprived others of their free will in the most offensive ways possible.

I believe the whole notion of attempted murder is bullshit; regardless of your intent, it really means you didn't get the job done. If you shoot, stab, punch, beat, poison, or do something else that almost, or could have, killed a person – it's just as bad as having killed them. Manslaughter is another bullshit charge; if you punch a drunk guy and he dies from a subsequent fall, he died because of your actions plain and simple.

Not guilty by reason of insanity... show me a person who kills a person who is sane? An action is an action, a crazy person who "wasn't aware of their actions" when they were killing, or trying to kill, a person should be punished just as harshly as the next douchebag.

If you're into threatening life with weapons to steal shit, I hope you like the taste of coconuts. If you fuck children or deprave them in some other twisted way (baiting/filming/photos/kid sex/animals/sexual acts of any kind), you're in for a very special kind of field trip. If you rape someone – start packing, you're going on a one-way vacation. If you straight up kill someone, hope you can paddle. No good behavior tab, no paroles, no conjugal sessions – you're forgiven, but goodbye, see ya, fuck off and let the rest of us get on with it.

The death penalty is wrong and is an ineffective deterrent. Who is anyone to claim the authority to take a life anyhow? A penal colony is the only morally justifiable way to punish murderers, attempted murderers, man slaughterers, people who threaten people with deadly force, pedophiles and rapists – because it removes these people (a demonstrated threat) from our society without eradicating their free will.

*Jail is big business. Big business in employing guards, construction contracts for new facilities, food catering contracts, inmate labor, furniture/amenities, maintenance contracts, and so on.

MENTAL ILLNESS

People fear the shit more than cancer and AIDS combined. I once mentioned to my old man that if he had to tell his friends his son was gay, for the sake of argument, or mentally ill, he'd pick gay if he had the choice. He didn't even hesitate in agreement; not in a malicious way, he just nodded and took the last bite of his apple; the guy's a fucking beauty.

Mental illness gets stuffed in the basement and attic of society debatably more than, or second to, the mentally disabled.

On any given day about 50 million Americans are suffering from some form of mental illness. Over 3 million Americans are schizophrenics and as many are manic-depressives. Over 30,000 Americans kill themselves every year; over 400,000 people end up getting treated for self-inflicted injuries. In the last century, more Americans died by their own doing than the total number of American soldiers who died in every armed conflict combined, and then some.

For all of the people traumatized "for life" after having seen a person jump out of the Trade Towers... what if you saw over three thousand people jump (not die in fast explosions and crumbling impacts, but take that ballsy leap) every month? A life is a life. There is nothing more tragic about a salesman jumping from a building because he can't take the pain of a flame than a salesman jumping from a building because he can't take the pain of life.

You can take a few days off of work when you have the flu, but not when you think you're having a mental breakdown. You can lie in bed for a month if a loved one dies, but not if you can't explain why you don't see the point in doing anything anymore. We rush to comfort a young person who has been in a traumatic accident or who suffers from a terminal illness, but not the weird kid who starves or cuts themself, or who has a host of emotional problems a person can have. Flowers, cards, pledges and marathons for the guy who can't eat chocolate bars, but jackshit for the secretary down the hall who hears voices and sees things crawling up the walls.

I don't mean to trivialize other illnesses and problems that people face. It's just that by ignoring, being ignorant of and uncompassionate towards an issue that destroys people's lives... it's a sign of how much we have to learn.

The worst part of mental illness is that it doesn't just affect those of us who just snap. Mental illness is also a prerequisite to a raft of life's circumstances – losing loved ones, getting sick or in an accident, taking drugs, stress at work or in general, having a lack of money, having a lack of education, and on and on it goes. It makes no sense that something that is so crippling and such a threat to all of us, is so misunderstood, not talked about, and not treated properly. There is a triad which is comprised of mental illness, drug abuse, and poverty. While all three human conditions can occur independently of each other, more often than not it is mental illness that leads to a mix of two or all three.

So what is mental illness? Mental illness is a disorder affecting mood and personality. People get mentally sick when they are in an unfavorable environment that causes their brain chemistry to misalign, if you will. Their thought processes, in an unfavorable environment, can literally change their chemical balances in their brain for the worse; kind of the opposite of when you're in a good situation and your mood, and take on life, improves. And sometimes people's brain chemistry misaligns naturally, and a person cannot function in their environment as a result. People with personality disorders use different traits (negativity, passivity, detachment, lying, obsession, etc.,) to cope with the burden of emotional difficulties in their life; the burden they don't know how to, or are unwilling to, face and resolve for good.

The homeless aren't so by choice. They are people who are sick, or suffer from drug addictions that have led to mental illness, or suffer mental illness that led to drug addictions. They are not people who are lazy. There is nothing lazy about struggling to find shelter where you won't be stabbed or raped, searching for food in a pile of garbage, or trying to find a place to take a dump in a concrete jungle. The homeless are the front line of mental illness.

There are more people who are genetically predisposed to mental illness who never develop it than those who do. Stress, especially when its onset is sudden, is probably the biggest trigger of mental illness. There will always be people who go a little funny, but stressful living conditions compound the problem. The real reason why mental illness springs up in so many people's lives isn't understood correctly.

Mental illness is a psychological reflex to a psychological or environmental conflict.

The depressed person is sad because there is something in their life (be it their job/spouse/friends/goals or purpose) that they know, deep down, is wrong and their mind is telling them (by literally forcing the person to close shop) to identify it and correct it. The person who is painfully introverted or superstitious has yet to acknowledge and identify their own will and sense of autonomy in life and is stuck in an endless cycle of self-rejection and doubt; the point of their abnormalities is to force them to overcome their fears and realize their true potential – the ability to demonstrate their desires and will.

A schizophrenic draws inward to the mind's subconscious and archetypes (another reality which they often project) because they are too poorly adapted to handle the demands of the world or a personal circumstance in life. The manic depressives simply suffer from severe mood swings which can lead to great personal insight and joy, but at the cost of a stable life and dangerously dark and depressed perceptions.

In the end, mental illness isn't even an illness. It's the mind's way of dealing with personal issues. There are as many contributing factors that lead to mental illness as there are types. Mental illness, because it forces people who suffer from it out of society or society's normal mode of thought and perception, has been the greatest contributor to humanity's creativity and ingenuity; however, even as I romanticize, it has also caused more pain and suffering because it is not understood well enough by the doctors who treat it, the patients trying to get better, and the people in society who pass judgment on it.

It's ironic that talking about problems to people is the best way to alleviate mental illness and yet it's the last thing anyone in society wants to talk about or give face time to. If everyone was cool and accepting of the mentally ill, most of the mentally ill would experience full and shorter recoveries in conjunction with current treatments.

MENTALLY DISABLED

It's a tough one. Just when you think you have it bad, you have to look at all of the people in the world who are born with any kind of mental or physical handicap, or people who become handicapped later in life. And just when you realize that those people have it hard, think about the people who care for them. And the reason why you probably have to think hard is that most people don't really see the handicapped or their helpers. Justly so, we hide them away. It's awkward being around them, seeing them, having to think about how unfortunate they are, how brutal life can be.

Tribal peoples would kill off individuals who were a burden. Most people usually murdered babies born with handicaps. A hundred years ago sterilization of people with genetic links to abnormalities (relatives with criminal backgrounds or mental and physical disabilities) had support and was legal in parts of the United States. Nazi Germany shot and gassed their lame ducks. Luckily we don't kill off disabled people anymore, and luckily there are good people who help to care for them. Society has made huge progress with disabled rights.

Today being blind, deaf, mute, or immobile, aside from the immature jokes and obvious physical obstacles, isn't a big deal; you can find work, friends, lovers, and generally fit in. And for those with mental handicaps, but who function at a modest level, there are good people and employers who welcome and bring these people in; help let them live the most normal life they can.

But there is a dark side to it all. Those who are bedridden and incommunicative. Those who are stuck at the mental capacity of a five year old. The kind of poor people who were deprived of oxygen at birth, or who developed in a polluted womb, or who have malformed chromosomes, who are grossly deformed and on and on it goes; society's real rejects. Consciousness trapped in useless or acutely limited brains and/or bodies. I hate it when people romanticize about these people; there is nothing special about them; they are tragedies. What is special is their perseverance and endurance, even if they are unaware of it. For all of the people in life who never come close to even imagining having the chance to go on a road trip, get laid, cook an amazing meal, fall in love, listen to amazing music, pick a like, any like... it's pretty sad.

Hope lies in two things. Medical advancements will one day be able to repair any condition, syndrome, or undesirable mental or physical impediment. I'm not saying that we're all going to be designer babies, but there's no reason why you shouldn't give a person the gift of being able to think like an adult, wipe their own ass, take a shower, drive a car, and live a long and healthy life.

The second is the only real hero I've ever met, and his life's work. It's the story of a good-looking young man from a prominent family who could have done whatever he wanted in life. And instead of living a life that most well-heeled country club kids go on to live, well, he invited two guys with intellectual disabilities to live with him. As the story goes, this young man found God while giving a retard a bath. And in time, this man conceived of and founded over a hundred communities worldwide for the world's most depraved and unwanted people.

Communities for these people to learn of, and receive, love. Communities where a blind autistic girl, who would smear her own shit on walls, could learn to have peace, happiness, and acceptance. The man's name is Jean Vanier. He's the real deal. He did and does what he does not in the name of religion or some other silly cause, although he is religious. He helps because he feels it inside and is not taught to, or encouraged to by some outside influence like a church or holy rule book. We need more Jean Vanier's in the world and they need more of our help; the people who open their homes and lives to the people society shuts out.

If you see these disadvantaged people, be kind and help them if you can. You might learn something about yourself in the process.

ABORTION & HOMOSEXUALITY

These are two issues used by politicians to gain power and distract people from urgent issues pertaining to governance. The people impacted by these issues aren't the people who object to them, but are, rather, the people who have been and are a part of these labels in society. These are issues of personal choice, as we will see more clearly in a bit. They are issues that are made into debates about a person's right to control what they want to do with themselves using their free will and choice, always based on religious morality. And when you take away a person's ability to choose in life, you're taking away their free will; par for the course with religion.

And as we've learned, free will is, coupled with having experiences, the whole point of being human. Take away a person's free will and you make a slave. So, first up, killing babies?

KILLING BABIES?

With it comes only one fundamental point of debate – it's really not about a woman's right to choose; we, regardless of sex, can choose anything, but if it's murder, there is a right and a wrong here. Is it murder? Is destroying an unborn organism that will one day be a human murder? If so, the whole choice thing goes out the window because a lot of us would like to murder newly born and grown people, but we can't; it's wrong because they're people, people who almost always don't want to be murdered. We can end the abortion debate forever if we can determine if abortion is actually murder.

To do that we need to define what a human is. A human breathes oxygen through its mouth and nose and into its lungs – a fetus doesn't. A human ingests food through its mouth – a fetus doesn't; this is not to say a disabled or injured person, or newborn baby or child isn't human because they need help eating and so on – it's to say that they are humans in need of help, not organisms in need of help to become human, as is the case for a fetus. A human reacts to, and interacts with, other humans on a conscious, interpersonal level – a fetus doesn't. It's key to understand that a fetus is striving to become human; it is not human. Whereas, once you're kicking and screaming, gasping for air, seeing the light, boom – you're a human.

Choosing to have an abortion should be a pretty simple yes or no matter; either the child is wanted or it is not; either circumstances permit a new child or they don't. Deciding on whether or not to terminate a pregnancy is not like deciding to put an offer in on a house, i.e., it shouldn't take half a year of your life. But just as I say that I think of the woman whose husband leaves her at seven months and would rather die than have his child; it's tough. Being human is tough; every story is unique. And that's why we can't make up these rules and laws that confine our choices and happiness in life like iron barriers. But luckily we can follow reason and guide our choices by that new moral... what is wrong if what you do or say doesn't hurt another person. If you consider a fetus a person, I can't help you. Me, I care more about the humans here. We can't even stick up for living humans let alone fetuses.

Canada is pretty good onabortion. If a woman needs one, she has full access and it's paid for by Heath Care, i.e., people who pay taxes; although she and her partner should pay for it themselves. And so as to protect her from potential shame or problems at home a woman doesn't need to notify her parents or spouse if she is having an abortion (and it would be against her right to privacy any other way). In Canada you can have an abortion leading up to five months of term, or unless the fetus endangers the mother's health after that (important in that a person with years of experience, love, time and money vested in them is more important than a fetus that can be replaced (and quickly forgotten) within months compared to an established human life). While a partial birth abortion is pretty rough to look at any way you cut it, given that the fetus is ready to become human, it's a sacrifice some have to make in order to preserve the sacredness of existing, established human life.

I don't mean to make light of the matter, but I think of the countless women who have gone through emotional turmoil at the hands of society's attitude towards abortion. Listen, it's not the end of the world. Shit happens. And most people who have abortions are better off in the end. But why?

Why do people have abortions? Because there are people who accidentally, or negligently, become pregnant and don't want to have a kid. Or you may be old and fear having complications, or you may not have enough money; whatever, it's not your fault and it's certainly not the end of the world. And if you bring a kid into the world who isn't wanted you usually end up with a person who feels unwanted, has a miserable go at life, and in the worst of cases makes life hard for others.

I was a party to an abortion once. Do I feel like my soul is going to burn when I die? Do I feel as though I helped to commit murder? Do I think of the face of my child that could have been? Fuck no. I think of how poor off I'd be today if I had had a child; how poor off the kid would be. And I also remind myself that if it was such a big deal, then how is it that I can create a new pregnancy every time I want to get laid or jack off? It was a learning experience in life – brought about by a girl's birth control being negated by a commonly prescribed antibiotic. Hardly reason enough to justify another person on the planet.

For the people who say that there are women who use abortion as a contraceptive, I say that yes, yes there are idiots among us; this is nothing new or surprising. A right is a right, no matter how many times you exercise it or not.

For all the pro-life people who cite the blind and deaf lady, Helen Keller, I have one name for you – Saddam Hussein. His mother was told to abort him. She didn't, almost died, and look how great that one turned out. It's about choice. We have the choice to choose to live by our own ideals. Tyranny is life lived by other people's ideals.

After we get the notion that killing a fetus isn't killing a human, the notion of forcing another person to have another person against their will is pretty fucked up. Fucked up and a waste of our time and energy. Are evangelicals going to have their way and have would-be aborting mothers confined, then strapped to tables and undergo Cesarean sections? And I'd like to know how many people at these pro-life rallies actually have adopted children? My point exactly.

Lastly, my dear pro-life people, stop it with this blame and shame game; stop taking your frustrations out on others under the pretence of morality; you are not perfect; no one gave you the gavel. Your God and his servant miscarriage are the biggest abortionists known to fetus. Nature, or your God, seems to discard what it doesn't want; why can't living humans?

Let's grow up as a species and start worrying, not about fetuses, about the actual kids and people already here with us who have no one to love and care for them.

Let it stand that a woman has the right to choose to kill a fetus, if it is one that grows inside her. A fetus is not a human being, but is an organism evolving towards such a state.

ASS BLASTING & RUG MUNCHING

Just when you think we're an advanced species, you have to look at the divisive issue of where and how people get off and love each other. Homosexuality isn't a real concern for well-adjusted, reasonable people today. Why is this an issue? Are gays hurting straight people in some way? I find overly-devout religious people to be a threat to my way of life, but I've never taken up a cause against them that tries to limit their rights to do and say what they please.

If we are going to get on as a species we need to understand that homosexuality has been around forever and will continue to be around. As such, we can deduce that it's actually a normal occurrence in life, in society; and if it's a regular occurrence that is consensual, what harm can be done? AIDS is a new disease, but women have been fond of women and men have been fond of men since hormones came into existence. And while AIDS is a new disease that predominantly affects gay people, in the West, a lot of heterosexual people died from small pox, tuberculosis, measles, malaria, and even infections. Homosexuality is prevalent in nature; when some animals can't find a mate, they try and score from a dude who is willing to offer up his ass for the sake of harmony in the herd. Strange, hilarious, but true.

There are two major reasons why homos get a bad rap. The first is religion. Many people believe people should live life according to a book, as opposed to their hearts. And because these books, which contain pages on how to kill people and prohibit gay love, well, people are afraid of anything gay because they are afraid of breaking the rules in the book and society's norms. These are weak-minded people who've never really thought for themselves.

The second reason is that most of us are straight and are afraid of what we don't know or what we don't want to be; it can be threatening. And so, thanks to a bunch of confused idiots, homophobia is born. As a result, we get a whole segment of the population, albeit a vast minority, feeling alienated, weird, and unloved. What the modern person knows is that they don't give a fuck about what other people do, so long as it doesn't affect them adversely. Weak-minded people are the people in our society who feel threatened by gays or anyone else who acts or thinks differently from them.

These same weak-minded people are those who feel threatened by homosexuals obtaining equal legal rights that acknowledge spousal rights and benefits; as if a bunch of cocksuckers gaining these rights and benefits will somehow lessen theirs. If a woman has been living with a woman for five years, doing the dishes with her, taking out the trash, paying bills, all of that shit – guess what – they deserve that same legal rights as a man and a woman who do the same shit. Equality, not tradition and convention.

As for homosexuals being married, I get them not being allowed to be wed in churches; it goes against the tenets, the faith, and the rule book. But a marriage also means and is defined as a union between two people. And even if it wasn't, two people should be able to be recognized by the law as legal partners; as gay as that sounds. But again, weak-minded people feel that the specialness of their married status is somehow diminished if gay people get to join the club; remember we all want to feel special, we all want love.

Should gays be allowed to adopt or have children? I think we touched on it earlier, but sure, any loving person should be allowed to take in an unwanted kid, or a kid whose parents think might be better off with someone else. Kids can adjust normally with same sex-parents, it's just that trouble arises when people or society judge gay parents or children from gay parents differently. Basically, if society gets over convention and homophobia, it won't matter who pays your bills – just as long as you're in a loving and stable home.

Gays in the military? Who gives a fuck? If you can shoot a gun and kill people, you can shoot a gun and kill people. If you can shoot a load all over another man's chest, you can probably shoot a gun and kill people.

THIS NOTE'S FOR YOU

I always used to think of art, in any capacity, as a flaky, meaningless pursuit. Art class was always a joke, but usually less so than the teachers themselves. What I saw as retarded people in colorful surroundings was actually a "Picasso." The whole notion of someone rolling around in or throwing paint at a canvas in exchange for press, accolades and obscene amounts of cash is, as I see it, ridiculous.

Art is meant to be a means for people to express themselves and their impressions of their surroundings, which can then be observed by others to relate to, learn from, or get some kind of emotional experience out of. The best artists report to us, through their creation, on the human condition. The most talented artists are the ones whose work is difficult to duplicate and even harder to imitate; and it's usually this art that is the most progressive and profound in nature. The best art helps us understand ourselves and our environment and helps to stimulate healing and new thought.

For me, I feel the pressure of a world where everything costs money and the reality of this makes the world a hard place; doable, but hard. The drive for money often brings out the worst in things, in people. For me, art has always been something that fights against the evils of the world by revealing truths and pleasure, although not always a combination of the two. Art can change ideals and free people to new ways of life through enlightenment; whereas corporate agendas and avaricious mind-sets, either intently or by nature, aim to suppress these nurturing qualities of art.

Modern art is revealing how our cultures, and most of the artists in them, are infected by the corporate-like influenza going around. For thousands of years even the most famous artists lived and died broke. The lucky ones made some money along the way, but died broke and/or insane. At some point, people realized you could bring great pleasure to people by revealing art to the public. Then, at some point, people realized you could make money revealing art to the public. And at a more recent point in our history, people realized that you can get into art for a career.

Art is now big business. It's gone from being something created for the sake of art and the artist, which could also be sold, on to something that can be made for money and all of its trappings. Even worse, art has turned into a means to help sell and promote ideas and products that art, in its essence, seeks to vanquish.

I don't think of the band KISS as really much of a band. That group was more of a marketing plan. The music, which is pretty shitty and meaningless, came second with that band. KISS was all about the filler – the image. Gene Simmons was a very shrewd marketer. He knew he could make it big if he could catch people's eyes first, instead of their ears. And it worked to the tune of about 90 million albums sold. Without the make-up for shock value, KISS would have been seen for what they really were – a really inferior version of Thin Lizzy. And they rode the strategy all the way to the bank with lunch-pails, action figures, a cartoon show, and endorsements. Every pop act/band/group/singer follows some element of the KISS strategy. In two hundred years time, what will people learn from listening to The Backstreet Boys, Britney Spears, Greenday, Kanye West, Kid Rock, or Nickelback? But good for them.

Television shows like *American Idol* and other spin-off flops are concocted to sell advertising and records – period. If the talent is good, all the better, but only rarely does a contestant end up with a career and, even then, it turns into the nightmarish formula and regiment as mentioned above.

When I worked for an art dealer in New York I was amazed to learn how artists were commissioned to crap-out hundreds of paintings for hotel renovations (a painting for every room). A painting done up in half an hour could be sold for hundreds. I remember having to pick up a piece from an artist, to be shown to a buyer later in the day. When I arrived the piece wasn't ready; about half finished. So I came back an hour later and it was done; asking price, $3,000. The New York art scene, from photographers to sculptors, left a really unfavorable impression on me. It was the stereotypical stuck up and pretentious vibe you'd imagine it to be. I'm all for people making as much as they can; but when that's the sole purpose of the art created... the art is usually shit and fails to serve its purpose.

The world of design has been going nowhere for a long time. The overall appearance of vehicles, homes, cars, furniture... anything really, hasn't changed that much. Crappy design and creativity is the reason there is always a new retro trend in our culture; because a lot of things were better back in the day. The new World Trade Center could have been used to showcase creative achievement, if not, more appropriately, a cemetery and memorial. It could have been used as a precedent in modern man's dedication to striving for the new and improved. And what did we get? Another building/office/shopping complex. The multi-floor revolving building in Dubai would have been cooler. The Great Pyramids are cooler.

Every time we make something that shapes how we live and the esthetic of our environment, we make a commitment to thinking a certain way for as long as what we have made is with us. Where are the new Buckminster Fullers or the people who know how to implement and integrate his ideas? Do we really want to work and live in the confines of modern day caves that we call offices and condos? Do we really need to keep building the same old boring shit just to make a buck? Right now that's where it's at. I think money and progress can go hand-in-hand. It's just a matter of who has the balls.

What takes a big dump in my mouth is when artists end up becoming spokespeople.

Paul McCartney helped make music about having a good time, falling in love, loving people, forgiveness, and basically songs that anyone can stand listening to. The guy has more money than Satan. Tickets to his shows average well over $100; usually $200-$250 for a good view. His music rights bring in the royalties that could buy whole African countries a cup of coffee a day for decades. Life has been good to the guy by rewarding him with talent, approving audiences, travel, luxury and all the good stuff. Then what does he do in his old age? He does fucking commercials for Fidelity Investments. He uses his name, face, and musical history to sell financial advice and plans. Why? He doesn't need the money, or the fame, or the ego boost. Why? Did he owe someone a favor? He made himself a salesman. He was used by a company to target older, financially-comfortable people to help invest in companies. Good job Paul.

I dropped my spoon in the cereal bowl one day when I saw a personal hero of mine, a real fucking rock star, Slash, whoring Volkswagens. I guess writing some of the biggest tunes ever, being in one of the most influential bands ever, touring the world, filling every vagina ever introduced to you, the yacht and hotel parties, the cash, the gift of talent... it wasn't enough. He had to add promoting Passats to his list of shit to do. The guy has nothing in common with the company or the people who drive its cars. But they plant his mug and image in their ad and presto – they get the Slash brand name recognition to help sell status symbols that pollute air and water and which are made in Mexico. The guy is a fucking legend, but that commercial made him look like a joke.

When I heard "Rock N' Roll" in a Cadillac ad I lost all the respect I had for Led Zeppelin and, sadly, the meaning of what their music meant to me faded as well.

A person's take on how art should be pursued and how it should be exploited is as subjective and open to interpretation as the whole subject of art is in its entirety. But to back my point up, art is, as it is supposed to, acting like a mirror in our culture, showing us just how consumed we are in this materialistic freak show.

ALIENS?

They're a favorite topic of mine. If anything, the notion of super powerful, intelligent and technologically sophisticated species is, at the very least, an outward projection of some people's hopes and desires for the human species. Because we can conceive of intelligent beings that travel faster than the speed of light, studying different planets, who are well-versed in all the knowledge of the universes, who live in peace amongst each other, who are probably peaceful with others, and so on... I believe this is a latent potential that we all possess. Some of us anyhow. I believe that we have the ability to one day be seen by other life forms on other planets, if they exist, as aliens. I've touched on this earlier by describing how, compared to other life in this world, we are indeed quite alien like. With time, evolution, and technological advancements we might one day have flying saucers of our own, if we don't already.

I believe science fiction is our species' projection of our potentials. How many tools do we have now that resemble things used in *Star Trek*? I use to hate *Star Trek*. Aside from all of the constant hostility between the humans and other civilizations (an example and projection of our primitive culture and enlightenment) I now realize what the show is all about - life beyond earth - doing and seeing more than we do and see now - the future - our potential and the potential of what we think might be out there.

But it's important to realize that before we can come close to becoming like the advanced "beings" in our science fiction novels and movies, we need to start thinking like advanced beings.

Do they exist? The evidence is overwhelming that there are things that fly in the sky in ways that modern engineering and technology cannot explain or replicate. The personal accounts of people who have had strange encounters with alien beings, both in person on land or in flying objects, is overwhelming. I have met reputable people who have seen UFOs but don't "go public" because the public associates anyone who speaks of aliens as crazy; because the public is dumb.

Of the perfectly sane people I've met who have seen these things, they all live in, or at the time of sighting happened to be in, remote areas. And of course they were in the middle of nowhere; you can't create a spectacle when there's no one around. These sane people are all uneasy with the subject because their experiences horrified them and called into question their certainty of the world around them. As for the certifiably unstable people who've had experience with Aliens and UFOs, my guess is an intelligent being would first appr-oach a person who's nuts simply for the fact that they would be more open to the bizarre, the different, and would less likely be afraid. But I'm just throwing out bullshit guesswork here.

The fact that Governments hide things from the people who give them the opportunity to even consider hiding something, is proof alone of how Governments are corrupt, keep people ignorant, and how people (the ones who accept and comply with Government secrecy) are stupid and worthy of such treatment.

If they do exist, here's why they wouldn't reveal themselves. Not be-cause people would riot or that civilization would crumble; although this would likely be the case. The fact is that the behavior of something changes once it realizes it is being observed. People act differently when kids, cops, friends, family - you name it - are around. If we knew for sure that Aliens existed and were watching us closely, we probably would get our shit together and evolve faster in every area of our existence. But that would be cheating things. The point is that we have to grow up on our own, of our own volition.

If there are aliens out there, chances are the first group of them were at one point in a situation similar to that of our species. And at some point they got their shit together, learned how to live longer, healthier, in peace and perfected space travel. And they would have had to have figured it out on their own, without the help of spaceships hovering over every major city to de-board and teach them the way.

I'm betting that we're not alone, but we'll never know until we can get off of this rock. If we don't, no biggie. It's a tragedy and a waste of the pain and suffering our species has endured to reach even our present state of de-velopment, but earth, and the people on it, aren't that significant in the big pic-ture of all that is. If we don't make it, the only thing that might care will be us. This is why it's so important that we all get along, realize we're all we've got, and try to produce things that make life easier using the gifts of consciousness, our bodies, intelligence and reason.

DEATH

It's a tough thing for people to deal with. The worst is when people die in accidents or at a young age. The permanence of someone being gone, no more, not around, never... it's harder to deal with and express than we could ever convey through our present means of communication; it's something that can only really be felt.

While it's a part of life, death is bullshit. It's not right that we should be born into a body and life that depends so much on closeness with others and be able to literally vanish at any given time. It's not right that lovers lose lovers, that parents lose children, children lose parents, and friends lose friends. It's not right that people get sick and suffer. There's no sugar coating. The only thing we can do is accept, keep moving, and heal somewhere in the process.

We die only because our bodies are fragile and are programmed to breakdown in time; everything in existence comes into it, then passes out of it – it's a law.

Death has helped our species evolve. With every generation born, information is passed on, learned, and more is added to the previous knowledge base through the new generation's experiences. When the old generation dies off, the younger generation asserts itself and imposes its newer ideals on the generation it creates. While this progress has been very slow, it has been rapidly increasing over just the last few hundred years; think of how much better life is now than it was a couple of thousand years ago? Imagine if some biblical prophet was still around telling us what to do? What a nightmare.

You have to realize that the whole universe is us and we are it; we are a part of it all. Death doesn't matter because we didn't do anything to deserve our lives in the first place. And the line about death revealing the absurdity of life couldn't be farther from the truth; death reveals the absurdity of how we live life.

WORK

I can't really speak to the subject. I've worked hard in life to avoid work; that's the hardest thing I've ever worked at. I had two paper routes as a kid; one for a major paper on Sundays and the other one was a freebee once a month. The Sunday paper always got delivered because my father would drive me in the early mornings. But the other paper always got thrown out, every bundle, most of the time; no one ever seemed to notice.

My summer jobs always made me miserable, with one exception. I got to work on a grain farm in Saskatchewan. The family I worked for was wonderful and the man I worked closely with left a favorably long-lasting impression on me. He taught me a lot about life just by being himself. And of course it was amazing to see the beauty of the Prairies, especially the sky at any time of day. It was a coming-of-age experience, except without the falling in love and boffing in a haystack with a local girl.

Other than that, after I flaked out of high school I worked at a car wash. I think I got canned for telling the supervisor to fuck off.

A few weeks after that I was accepted into a comedy school. Of course I was expelled a couple of months in for the usual bullshit; farting too frequently and too loudly and always making a joke out of everything.

Upon my dismissal, I published an issue of a comedy magazine and funded it with the help of an aunt and washing cars in my parents' backyard; not to brag. I made a shitload of cash off of the commercials. Before the union fucked everything up and the Canadian dollar gained more parity with the U.S., landing a U.S. national commercial was a big deal. Landing $35,000 for one of my last big ones funded a fateful year for me in New York. I blew it all on debauchery. In fact, most of the money I made off of commercials was spent on lavish meals, cigarettes, booze, women and travel; that's why I had to go to my aunt for the magazine cash.

I've always been reckless with money because I have such a distain for the whole concept of it; I know we need to work and that money measures the success of our work, but I'm just not wired for it. Pieces of paper determining who eats what and who lives where. I hate it. But I'm all too cognizant of the fact that it's the way things are.

When I was forced to do something with my life I went to college and got a degree in advertising; a subject of considerable interest because of my gloriously unsuccessful attempts to land ads for the magazine and because of Bill Hicks

During college I worked the box office at a comedy club and, with the help of the doormen, raped the shit out of the till. On my end, most of it went towards buying books, food, concert tickets, and attending conferences and speaking engagements. The doormen used their take for the mundane... diapers, car payments, gas, presents for children and probably to get fucked up. A lesson in necessity was learned. I should mention that a manager was fired for suspected theft. I know he wasn't even close to culpable, but I also know our skimming operation could not have thrown the books off; our system was off the books and the amount he was held accountable for wasn't even close to our numbers; it was way too low. If this book makes me any dough, I'll cut the owner of the club a check for sure; I would not have made it without his help.

I did a summer internship a year into the program and fucked the dog as much as possible. My internship at the end of the program was the most wasted six weeks of my life. All I did was surf the Net and bullshit with the guy who shared my office; there just wasn't any work to do. The office was at the end of the hall by the exit, which afforded me constant smoke breaks, late arrivals and early exits. I didn't fit in at all because I didn't, and couldn't, take the job and office culture seriously. The best part was at the end of the internship I was offered a job! You can't make this shit up!

So I took the summer off to bang a broad who was a really cool hippie chick. By September I had to appease my old man by getting a job with an ad agency. He got me in the door through one of his contacts and I walked out the door six weeks later for the usual reasons. It was a good thing, too, because I got my old job back at the box office and was making more cash than I would have at the ad agency, working a fraction of the hours.

I eventually got canned from the box office gig when I showed up to work hammered one St. Patty's day. It was almost intentional, and I knew I had to move on in life. Plus the party was awesome that day. A couple of months later I ended up bussing at a buddy's bar and eventually bartended there. It was a great fucking job and I have the liquid nitrogen scars to prove it.

With time and some serious introspection, I got out of the bar scene. I blame leaving the life of easy money and women on this book and a breakup with a chick I had been dating for two and half years. Working for 8-12 hours with the routine of mass alcohol consumption and the subsequent hangovers, conjoined with meeting the constant needs of another person, for me, leaves no room for inspiration, discovery or creativity.

So I bailed and liquidated my assets: a chair and a dresser a friend gave me. Then, like divine intervention, I met a man and his wife while drowning my sorrows in a steak. We got to talking and he offered me a job in something that was of actual interest to me. It would give me cash and the time I needed to finish this book. Cool. And then he stopped taking my calls. I was fucked. Broke, no woman and no prospects. But I did have time on my hands and no more obstacles to distract me from finishing this glorious piece of shit.

So what did I do? I called up my credit card company and the morons gave me an extra $7,000. With it, I was able to finish the book and position myself to publish. And of course I thank my family (with a couple of exceptions) and friends for whatever support and kindness they gave me. Nothing ever gets done without other people helping out in ways both seen and unseen. In the end I got back into bartending and disc jockeying at a tittie bar to pay for this book. And, of course, I got back with the ex for a while.

I guess you have to do what you have to do to get by. Just try and do something you want to do. Take risks. Work hard at what you're good at and hopefully you like what you're good at. Read the next bit titled Value Added. Don't exploit your workers – they'll steal less from you in return. If you steal, return it when you can and only steal when its essential and when it doesn't hurt a person. Don't be one of those dipshits who's proud to have an office fob or swipe card. Don't be one of those fucking douchebags who gets excited by an expensed meal, or a gift basket, or having a personalized business card. If you have to work five days in exchange for two days off – do something you could look back on and say "ya, I spent 45 years doing work that meant something to me."

VALUE ADDED

If we want shit more peaceful, fun, knowledgeable, advanced and sustainable, we have to look at what kind of value the people around us add.

Most of us stumble into what we do for a living by convenience, fluke, through a friend, or an unexpected opportunity. Sometimes we're forced into something by unfavorable circumstances or people. If you're lucky you get to do what you love; you're even more fortunate if your love helps others in some way.

We need to start looking at what we do with our lives and the short time we get to play with.

We need more good doctors, nurses, paramedics, firefighters, and rescue workers. We don't need more cops, but we do need the ones we have to be good and to help those who need it. We need more scientists and researchers to explore, invent, and find ways to improve our knowledge base and lives in general. We need more engineers to improve everything from infrastructure to travel. We need people who understand nature and can help us exist with it in harmony. We need people who can grow food and manufacture resources in ways never imagined. We need people who know how to grow great drugs and distil the finest spirits. We need people who know how to build the infrastructure needed to create all of the good ideas people come up with. We need people who can help teach kids about life and inspire them to do something positive with it.

We need better art and roller coasters with faster lines for fuck's sake.

What we desperately need less of is politicians, bankers, accountants, brokers and agents of any stripe, lawyers, marketers, media planners, copywriters, people in PR, clothing companies, lobbyists and any other racket profession.

ACT II

INTRODUCTION

I was born in Canada. A place with a tenth of the population and the same kind of living standards as the States, but with fewer mega malls, more potholes, fewer murders, more taxes, and fewer racial problems. And Canada has hockey; a sport more Americans follow less closely than cricket.

Our biggest national divide, in my opinion, is over a predominantly French speaking province and its desire to separate from the rest of Canada. A former French prime minister made Canada an officially bilingual country. Now we have one side of a box of cereal in English and the other side in French and you have to hear pilots and stewardesses make their announcements twice, but in one language you can't understand; even if you're flying from Vancouver to China. That same prime minister failed to have the French province sign the constitution with the rest of Canada.

The other divide could be our Native population's disputes over land, tax, and human rights abuses; all of which, in my opinion, are well-founded, but get less press because they have less political influence.

Conversely, the Sates has a slew of contentious divides: religion, abortion, gays, race, healthcare, money, extreme poverty, housing, corrupt politicians, erosion of supreme laws, immigration, war, the military, taxes, drugs, and so on. Not that Canada doesn't grapple with these matters, but the extent to which they seem to pit people against one another down South is, I guess, more amplified.

Canada has always had the luxury of being geopolitically insulated on account of being relatively close, friendly, and, obviously, harmless to the States. As a kid, whenever the subject of war came up, everyone would joke that Canada could never be attacked because we had the States so close by. Canada has reaped all the benefits of a First World nation because we've had such a close and undefended trading border with the world's largest economic and military empire. I'll piss off a lot of Canadians by saying as much, but when it comes down to it, it's the truth. Most of all, Canada is an example of what a trade relationship based on mutual respect (for the most part) and not exploitation, coupled with an educated populous, can create – a pretty fucking great place to be born.

Me, I always envied the States. The story of the Founding Fathers, its birth as a nation, the triumph over slavery and the civil war, its rise to a world superpower in my parents' lifetime... the States just has a better story than Canada. Canada is the place where all of the pussy's and people who wouldn't stand up against oppression fled to; although Canadians did hit above their weight in both World Wars (as many Americans are unaware of). But no, for me, I've always had a fascination with, and admiration for, The United States of America. I'll make it my permanent home eventually; it's been a dream of mine since I was a kid. I've always wanted to live where the action was.

I also owe my existence as I know it to the ideals of the States. My Grandfather immigrated to Ellis Island as a young boy with his Mother and Grandmother from present day Israel, then Palestine. Like most, if not all immigrants, they came with nothing because the land they came from (originally Lebanon) had nothing to give them. They weren't looking for a hand-out, just a hand-up in the form of a job. My Grandfather grew up in Jersey and went on to become an employee of the U.S. Government at the very port of entry that granted him and his family freedom. As a linguist, he employed his skills as an interpreter for U.S. Customs and Immigration. He was eventually posted in Canada. After fathering eight girls in his country of assignment, he finally fathered a ninth child – a boy, my old man.

The poor bastard lost his job when he gave some friends his working papers so they could travel in the States on their honeymoon. He died young at 57, broke and left behind a wife with nine kids to tend to. The American Dream kicked in when my old man made a success of himself and went on to spoil his kids. My greatest gift out of this whole story, aside from a life of privilege... was becoming a naturalized U.S. citizen.

Am I a real American? Yes. To me though, being American is a state of mind. When I was first issued my citizenship I didn't know what I would do with it or what it all meant, but I knew it had to be for something. Everybody was telling me how great it was that I could choose to work in the States if I wanted, but I hate work, working, and anything I don't want to do. I just knew on the drive back from Buffalo that the whole process meant something.

Now that American influence is giving way to rising powers in the East, an election was debatably stolen, Americans are becoming unemployed and indebted in vast numbers, poverty is getting worse, the Constitution is being ignored, wars are being fought on bogus pretenses, bombs are dropped without the consent of Congress, a kind of feudalism is drawing a concealed carriage of socialism and fascism, suicides and domestic violence are up, people are armed and agitated... it seems like a good time to address all of this with a call to action. Since no one else is making a real attempt, I thought I'd give it a go.

The rest of the book deals with some pretty serious social, economic, and political matters of great importance. Most people 30 and under have next to no awareness about them, and those who do don't really care; and this is why things are getting so bad – people aren't tuned in en mass. All I can do is try and explain things as simply as possible, as I've done with everything in the book so far. Hopefully I can spark your interest and concern so that you'll learn more for yourself and take action when the time is right.

~

For those who will say, "who does this Naturalized Canadian think he is to comment on The United States of America?"... I've got a good one for you:

The 44th President of The United States of America was born in the 50th State; an archipelago in the migrating pattern of the humpback whale, some 2,400 miles from mainland America. Going even further, and farther, the 44th president spent his formative years residing in Indonesia, a country just due north of Australia.

WHAT MAKES AMERICA GREAT & WHY THE IDEA MUST PREVAIL

The United States of America is more an idea than it is a country. It is, by virtue of its many states, just a bunch of small countries unified by core ideals. The people of the state of Maine have nothing more in common with the people of the state of Texas than do the people of the province of Ontario. People of both states are united by the idea of freedom and the right to control their lives and Government right down to the local level; at least that's what the Founders had in mind, but I doubt it's what, if anything does, unites anybody while walking down the street.

The Founding Fathers were the smartest, most enlightened group of men ever assembled in the history of our species. They believed that it was the right of people to be able to live their lives as free people; that a person should be able to embark on the pursuit of happiness without interference from oppressive leadership, taxation and wars. They knew they were ahead of their time and couldn't do it all at once (freeing slaves, women's rights and so on), but they knew they could establish a country based on an idea that could make it possible in time.

The greatest thing they created was a political system that could limit the size and power of Government by branching out its power structures and using each branch to effectively limit the others respective powers.

These men, the Founders, were well aware that lands ruled by men with unrestrained powers and allegiances were doomed. They knew that people were naturally inclined towards democracy, but that their true will could always be overthrown by a few men. They knew that only in a land where people actually governed themselves based on the rule of law could freedom persist, and that when the power of the people was diminished or lost, on account of a system that was susceptible to the likes of these predatory "few people," tyranny would ensue.

They knew that wars were a burden and that empires always fall. They knew that monopolies were dangerous to business and Government. They viewed excessive taxation as a robbery of the people. They were also men who hated being told what to do by a king who had little or no regard for their say in the matter.

So they conspired to create a land with responsible Government run by the people, for the people. The idea gave us timeless concepts like a Bill of Rights and a Constitution that would ensure a healthy and transparent government and the protection of individual rights. The Constitution would also keep the powers of Government in check; to stave off would-be tyrants.

And this land went on to generate the most prosperity, freedom, and innovation in the history of our species.

But this idea was really just an experiment. An experiment that allowed people to capitalize on their ideas, work, and free will to make life better for themselves and, in turn, others. It could only succeed as well as the people could be in control of it; their Government and their personal freedom.

Weak leadership, undedicated politicians (and the collusive banking and corporate interests that support them), as well as the many Americans ignorant to the gift this country affords them, are ruining this experiment. If the present course and trend of events continues, we're going to end up with a system run by a few powerful people and a progressively invasive Government; the same kind of scenario the Founding Fathers fought to get away from.

IS AMERICA A CHRISTIAN NATION FOUNDED ON JUDEO-CHRISTIAN "PRINCIPLES"?

It's a country with a bunch of Christians who reside in it. It can't be said enough. America is a country that was founded by a majority of men who were not staunch Christians. Most of the Founding Fathers were Deists and many attended church to keep up appearances. They opted for a secular state because only through secularity could they form a country based on reason, freedom, and the right of the people to have Government for the people, by the people; not Government for the people, influenced and dictated to by the religiously connected and/or religious authorities.

America is not founded on Judeo-Christian laws or morals. This whole business of America being based on the Ten Commandments is bullshit. Murder and stealing were morally forbidden for thousands of years before either Abraham or Jesus were dirty thoughts. I can see of nowhere in the Bill of Rights or the Constitution where an American is obligated to: not believe in more than one God, to not make idols (images of other gods or things of worship), to honor their parents, to not cheat on their spouses, to not want to bang their neighbors wife, to not want the stuff a neighbor owns, not take some God's name in vain, or to have a Holy Day. As for the bearing false witness part, in our justice system we have a thing called perjury (a concept that's also been around before Abraham and Jesus) which is a crime punishable by a justice system.

And let it be clear – the people who claim America is going through hard times because their God is angry over its citizens having, and being permitted to have, abortions, the ability to consume pornography and drugs, or the choice to pursue a homosexual lifestyle... suffer from the same kind of delusions as the people of primitive cultures who believed they had droughts because they weren't sacrificing (murdering) enough people in reverence to their God.

Both mind-sets are affected by psychotic thought processes, i.e., they're fucking nuts. And it should be pointed out that the individuals and groups who claim abortions, porn, drugs and fags are disgruntling their God, well, they always fail to mention the wars. People make their lives either easy or hard for one another. People who can't accept this have to look for an imaginary parent in the sky to reassure them that they don't have control over their lives; they haven't crossed that psychological threshold into adulthood.

No, America is not a Christian country and never has been. The God we trust in is the higher image of perfection that we must aspire towards becoming, or emulate.

EDUCATION

Growing up, the smart kids are the losers. It's only later in life that perceived roles are reversed. I loved the social aspect of school and the few classes I had with cool teachers and hot chicks. Being from a privileged family, I never gave a shit about school. I just figured, like a fucking idiot, that I'd go to university and end up making a lot of dough.

Having the opportunities to attend the schools I went to gave me several advantages that I didn't even know I was benefiting from. I always had field trips, motivated teachers, the best books, amazing facilities, and a solid curriculum. Being around kids who came from money exposed me and everyone to educated adults, nice homes and cottages, and exposure to decorum.

The kids who didn't come from money and were funded on academic or athletic scholarships enjoyed all the same benefits. In my early grade school years I remember one kid getting made fun of because his dad was a cab driver; kids, regardless of what their parents earn, can be cruel. Fucking brutal. Here's a kid going to a great school because his old man wants the best for his kid – better than his old man gave him. And what does he get? A bunch of kids teasing his kid.

As I got older, no one ever thought they were any better than public school kids; at least not any of my friends. And besides, most public school kids were cooler to hang out with anyways. But, as is understandable, a lot of them resented us.

I spent most of high school trying to not get caught smoking, chewing tobacco, masturbating, drinking, being up late, or trying to score blow jobs, while being oblivious to the opportunity I was wasting. But I got a wake-up call.

I realized the advantages a solid education gives you when I attended a public school. The public school I was zoned for was a joke next to the private school I had previously attended. The classrooms and hallways were run-down; the janitor was dragged out in handcuffs one day for dealing. The textbooks were mangled, and a lot of reading material was photocopied. I'm trying to think if there was a cafeteria? If so, I never went. The gym was in decent shape, but the few teams that existed were only available because a few teachers volunteered; most teachers were there to meet the minimum contractual obligation that rewarded a pension. Some of the teachers I had weren't fit to be teaching; they were unintelligent, uninspired, and there because they were unemployable in any private sector. The library was small and dated. All of this at what was supposedly a more academic school in the system.

Like any school, there were competent and engaged teachers and administrators; but this only served as patchwork. The course material and work offered to the kids was a fucking joke. After the first month, from an educational standpoint, the meaning of preparatory school sunk in.

The kids who wanted to do more with their lives, like get out of public housing, went on to university. For the clowns, potheads, and gang members – I dunno? Most of the kids from private school that I know of didn't go on to do a hell of a lot either, but the point is they had a huge leg up on most kids. I ended up going to class that year whenever I felt like it; most of the teachers knew I wasn't there seriously.

In the end I didn't write my exams and I didn't complete enough of the university prerequisite courses to do a hell of a lot. However, I did apply to Harvard on a lark, only to get fucked up the night before the SATs and sleep through the morning testing.

But good for me.

I've never been to an American school. I hear the universities are excellent. For $30,000-$50,000 a year they'd better be. I hear good things about many of the state schools. Higher education makes for a more skilled and productive civilization, less crime, and fewer kids. I do hear that many of the public schools are unfit environments for learning.

I do know that education isn't a concern, and shouldn't be of any concern, to any Government. Certainly states and municipalities shouldn't be in on how and what kids learn. Where a person goes to school and what they learn should be up to teachers and parents. Standardized learning hurts kids who learn differently, as well as those who might be gifted, and results in cookie-cutter minds. But this is what happens when you have one size fits all, publicly-funded education. You have a system that's concerned with meeting the standards of regulations and not the standards of quality and individuals. To top it all off, people, most importantly kids, don't respect what they don't directly pay for.

Schools should be maintained by the communities that use them. Parents should pay for their books (at wholesale and used prices), should chip in for field trips, cover the costs of maintaining the school and paying teachers' salaries. Maybe then there'd be pride in more schools and a desire to get something out of them. For the parents who genuinely couldn't afford $3,000-$5,000 (about what is required without a bureaucracy) to send their child to school, that's where charity drives and endowments come in. You find the resources from those who are willing to contribute them, instead of forcing people to give their money to a "system" to redistribute for them. Bureaucracies have been churning out some of the least capable minds to the tune of $8,000-$12,000 a head, per year. Do you really think more money is going to solve the problem here? It won't. We need to stop paying income taxes and use the savings to buy and create the education we want for kids. And I guarantee you that parents would become more involved and interested with their kids' academics if money was coming out of their savings directly, and not silently off of a paycheck.

HOUSING

We all need a place to live. Some of us live in places that aren't as nice as we could afford and some of us live in places that are nicer than we can afford. Some of us live in shopping carts, boxes, tents, tunnels, under bridges and on or under vents.

Demand for housing determines the availability and quality of housing. If prices are too high, people live in other places, or prices are lowered to encourage sales and rentals. For the people who have to move farther away from work to find housing that they can afford, so be it. If the commute is a problem, find a job that can afford you closer accommodations, or find another place to work. A short commute is not a right.

When people can't afford housing in a particular market, a new market is created elsewhere to meet their needs and budgets. This new market may consist of cheaper, smaller housing or housing built on less expensive land. In any event, the new market is created to meet the demands of people who cannot acquire housing in other markets.

When people can't afford housing at all, they should move into charity communities. If they are mentally ill or on drugs, shelters or need-specific charity communities it is.

WHY RENT CONTROL IS WRONG

Rent control aims to offer affordable housing to people who shouldn't be, or might not be able to afford, living in a certain building or area. It's a communistic measure that, 1. adversely affects economies and, 2. removes individuals (in this case the people who own/build/maintain property) personal choices and freedoms.

Rent control has a negative impact on a free market. If a property is forcibly undervalued (on account of capped/controlled rent), the surrounding properties are, as a direct result, undervalued. Price controls can't determine the value of things as well as consumers.

Who is a Government, municipality, or bureaucracy to tell a person what they can earn off of their property? Who is a Government, municipality, or bureaucracy to tell a person who can live on their property?

WHY HOUSING PROJECTS DON'T WORK

Housing projects are among some of the more honorable failures undertaken by Governments. The idea of giving people a free place to live sounds nice. In addition to the reality that it costs taxpayer money to put up and maintain these "free" accommodations, it doesn't work.

You'd like to think a person given something as nice as an apartment would be eternally grateful for, and respectful of the place. People don't take care of things that come for nothing. Housing projects always turn into the rundown, neglected shitholes they are because there is no incentive to reinvest in, and maintain, them.

ENERGY

When I started driving back in the 90s, gas cost anywhere from $00.38 a liter to $00.45 cents. In the States gas was running anywhere from $1.10-$1.50 a gallon. I drove a 1989 Chevy Lumina mini-van; even with dents, rust, one existing wiper blade, no hubcaps and a bumper sticker that rather boldly proclaimed "Quilting Forever, Housework Whenever," I managed to get laid. It cost about $28 to fill it. A pack of smokes cost about $4 dollars then. A domestic case of beer cost $25-$27. A McChicken combo, $4.50 something. Minimum wage was less than $7.00.

I knew, even at 16, that the whole economy depended on people making cash and spending it. If people didn't spend money, things wouldn't sell, businesses wouldn't be busy, and the economy would slow down. Gas was cheap, and so was the cost of travel. Cheap gas made it possible for globalization; making crap on the other side of the world was economically viable because the cost of energy to manufacture and transport goods was, like the cost of $80 all-in for a road trip to NYC - totally manageable.

But then a few years later gas went up to over fifty cents and then sixty. It stung a bit. Minimum wage went up a bit, but smokes were now more like $7.00 a pack. Beer shot up to $30.00 and McDonald's was pushing $6.00 for a hangover meal. Things were getting pricy, but everyone was working and prospering, so you just went about your day.

Then a real game-changer happened. Gas prices shot up so much that gas stations couldn't post the price on their signs. All of the signs only had three number spaces on them. And one magical night, all of the signs in town read $0.00. It didn't mean free gas. It meant gas cost $102.4 cents a liter. Eventually that number rose to $134.4.

All the talk on the street was about the rising cost in heating bills, groceries, travel, goods, you name it. A trip that would have cost me $70 something in gas was now well over $200.00. I stopped driving to New York. High oil prices cost New York's bars, record stores, cabs, deli's, sidewalk merchants, and dim sum joints over $5,000 of my business over the next while. Smokes cost over $10.00 a pack. Beer was well over $30.00 a case and the McChicken was over $6.00. The minimum wage, a little over $7.00. Prices were going up everywhere. It hit me that I had a lot less to spend. The money I did have, I was spending less of.

And so, I wondered, if I was spending less, was everyone else following suit? I didn't have a house or hydro and heating bills to pay for. I had no kids to drive around, feed, cloth, and so on. For the people that had these responsibilities, I couldn't help but think about how they were getting by with having to pay more for everything.

I'm not a seer, but as I suspected the economy came tumbling down; albeit, harder than I thought. When I asked knowledgeable people if it had anything to do with exorbitant gas prices, they all looked at me in amusement and blabbed on about big banks, bad assets, sub-prime mortgages and everything else they were reading in newspapers. But when gas went down to $00.83 cents a litre in the midst of the calamity, I made the connection: The cheaper the gas, the greater the economic activity, but the more expensive the gas, the less economic activity that can take place. The recent drop in gas prices was a result of less economic production in a recession.

This line of thinking states that as soon as the economy gets going again, oil prices will spike again on account of a stronger demand for a limited resource, and that when they do the economy will inevitably fall back into recession on account of the increased cost to produce/move goods and services. Sure enough, as of this writing, and about a year after the crisis with everyone feeling confident again (at least in Canada), gas has tweaked back up to $1.00. The days of cheap oil are gone.

But why? Why does the oil cost so much some days and less on others? Is it a conspiracy by global industrialists to drain the wealth of the nations? There's oil all over the world. There is more oil in Canada than the Middle East. As a kid I was told there was enough oil to last over 200 years before we had to worry.

About a year ago I found a book entitled, *Why Your World is About to Get a Whole Lot Smaller*. I hate it when people read a book and then claim to have all the answers, but the man who wrote it was a guy who predicted I was going to stop driving to New York at a time when I would have laughed off such a prognostication.

In the book he clearly demonstrates how globalization is dependent on cheap oil. But the point of the book is that we've reached the end of cheap oil. The easily accessed crude in the Middle East isn't coming out the ground as fast as it used to. And with the explosion of progress in developing countries, well, we have more people drinking from the same well. What's worse is that for all of the oil the world is consuming, oil companies aren't finding substantial new reserves.

So are we out of oil? No. But the proven reserves of oil we do have available cost a lot of money to get out of the ground. Conventional oil wells can supply the world during slow progress at a $2.00 a gallon, but if the world economy picks up pace and gets thirsty, it has to use expensive oil to make up for the lack of production in more cost-effective oil fields.

In essence, if we want to supply the oil demands of a strong economy, gas has to be expensive to cover the costs of drilling in places like tar sands and miles under the ocean. To put it in perspective, for every 1 Btu of energy expended through oil extraction in the Canadian tar sands, you get a return of 3 Btus. However, in the Middle East, for every 1 Btu of energy expended in the extraction process, you get 100 Btus of energy. Clearly, Middle Eastern oil is much more profitable. But, if gas costs $4.00 a gallon, or $150-$200 a barrel, the production of oil in Canada becomes profitable. And at those prices, the trade of goods halfway around the world doesn't make sense because of the increased manufacturing and transport costs; unless you want to pay more for them.

There are things in the book I don't agree with like, for instance, his support for carbon taxes and his assertion that sub-prime mortgages didn't contribute to the global crisis, citing Germany and Japan as examples. Carbon taxes are just that, a tax on something we have no way of getting around. A carbon tax will make Governments and a small number of people very wealthy, at the majority's expense, and will do little to cut back emissions; new technology, not penalties, will reduce emissions. While a housing bubble in Cleveland didn't directly affect the economies of Germany and Japan, it rattled America's, which reverberated across the oceans. Over-leveraged German banks and Japan's stagnation for close to twenty years were their respective economic tipping points.

The facts show that the global economy was gang-tackled by oil prices, inflation, unsound money, ridiculously loose credit, leveraged banks, and dangerous investments. There is a direct link to cheap oil and lower inflation, as cheap oil keeps the prices of things down. However, easy money and easy credit always drives debt and inflation upwards – creating bubbles that have to burst, regardless of the cost of oil. Expensive oil made the bubble that would have burst on its own, burst a lot sooner.

What we do know for sure is that we have an oil problem. Better efficiency and electric cars aren't going to solve the problem. Fuel efficiency, counter intuitively, drives up consumption. Electric cars will strain power grids that are already strained. Nuclear power plants are expensive, take a long time to build, and create dangerous waste. Solar and wind power is a drop in the bucket. Ethanol require gas to produce and is profligately inefficient. Offshore drilling is expensive, slow to set up, recently extremely unpopular, and a lot of the platforms always seem to be built in places that hurricanes have a propensity to frequent. We're going to be driving and flying less - or paying much more to do so.

And we're going to see more and more recessions.

The global trade we have now is going to cost a lot more if barrels of oil cost $125-$200. If people can't afford those prices, or businesses lose a competitive edge because of pricy gas, then we'll probably see more local trade. To learn more, read the book.

Is there a solution to the energy problems we face? Absolutely. People. People need to literally reinvent the concept of the combustion engine. Is it still relevant? Is there a better concept? Is there a limitless, powerful, clean source of energy and power that we haven't thought of? Definitely. I just think it's going to take a lot of scraping by on the energy sources we're all using until we take the next big leap in technology to get there.

FOOD

"I don't get it? How is my finishing everything on my plate going to help out someone starving on the other side of the world?"

– Unknown comic in Toronto

We waste a lot of it. Eat a lot of it that's poor in quality. And spend a lot of energy producing it. Why? Because the human stomach is a greedy motherfucker. It never stays full for more than a few hours.

We need food to replace the energy we expend. It doesn't have to look, smell, or taste good to get the job done. It just has to have calories. The more nutrition with those calories, the healthier the food. If you don't know what healthy food is, go plug your brain in. If you're feeding your family fast-food every day, here's a brilliant concept – take the $20-$30 you spend on burgers and fries and buy a loaf of bread, some fresh cold cuts, a jar of mayo, some tomatoes, lettuce and splurge on a jug of milk and some soup. Do that and think hard about having any more children; if not for your wallet and family's diet, do it for me.

We all know processed foods aren't the healthiest. We know a lot of our meat comes from some pretty nasty production lines. We know it's ridiculous to transport food all over the world, using gasoline and other chemicals in the process, for the sake of variety. And we know that genetically modified food might not be safe. So what can you do if you're concerned?

Market forces, baby. Buy what you want and avoid what you don't want. I eat McDonald's once a year when I'm severely hungover and someone offers to buy it; and more importantly, exerts the effort to go and buy it. I stopped eating fast food on road trips a while back; now I stop at a local restaurant if I have the time, or pack a few highly caloric bananas to throw down along the way. I eat out a lot, which is a reason I'm always broke. But I always eat well. When I do grocery shop I try and go to markets. There, I support the little local guy. My meat guy is supplied by independent farmers who use old-school farming practices; no drugs, clean kills, and herd sizes that aren't detrimental to the soil and water table. I've switched to organic fruits and vegetables because I know the damage that fertilizers and pesticides inflict on the Great Lakes; the source of my water for most of the year.

Speaking of water, I never buy the bottled stuff because most of it is just filtered tap water and the plastic waste is a joke. I don't buy much seafood anymore because most of the fish stocks are in trouble, and even the ones that aren't are still toxic; toxic, by my standards anyhow. The seafood I do love like lobster, crab, shrimp, oysters, and mussels, I consume much less of.

I don't complain about the bad food everywhere. I simply buy the stuff that's most appealing to me. If you don't like it, don't buy it.

As for vegetarians, vegans, fish-only's, eggs and cheese-ok's, and every other diet preference, all I can say is that they're great if they work for the people who opt for them. Many people with these dietary preferences proclaim "you wouldn't eat that if you had to kill it yourself and knew what you were doing to that animal." And I always tell them, "I would if I was hungry."

Life feeds on life. The grass eats the sun and the soil. The cow eats the grass, takes a dump and feeds the soil. The cow also gets eaten by me and I, too, feed the soil when a truck sprays my dump over a field. It's a holy symbiosis. Life feeding on life.

All of this said, it would be cool if one day we had the option of a meal in a pill replacement, or a meal in a bowl of vitamin and nutrient-fortified gush.

GUNS

Gun-control lobbyists, anti-gun activists, and other people of the mindset that guns are a threat to society, fail to understand a simple concept. Guns are the cornerstone of a free society. Guns are what keep society free. Every asshole that ever ruined and plundered a nation, achieved the ability to do so by disarming the obstacle to his unlimited power – the people. An unarmed people can't fight against oppression when their oppressors can shoot them down.

The United States of America is a revolutionary nation, born from the end of a barrel, by men who would have been executed had they not prevailed. Guns helped found the country and they will help keep its foundation intact. It's as simple as that.

Guns are a means for people to defend themselves and their property. How can genocide occur, if the ethnicities targeted for slaughter own guns? Do you think the Communist Party in China would have the ability to crack down on people like it does if, say, 100,000,000 were armed and could fight for, or against, things like democratic political parties, freedom of speech, land ownership and confiscation, a free press and Internet, or human rights? Martial arts were born out of Chinese peasants needing to defend themselves against the powers that be; the same powers that forbid the peasants to own weapons.

For people who think we've evolved out of ever having to worry about Government violence, or that we're too civilized now to have to worry about the kinds of atrocities people have endured from their leaders in the past, I suggest you re-read the part about The Shadow. History has a nasty record that shows us whenever a tyrant takes control of a group of people, whether by consent or through force, one of the first things he does is disarm the people.

There is nothing like a well-armed populous to keep a Government in check. And there is nothing more cruel and dangerous than an armed Government ruling an unarmed, helpless populous.

The right to own guns for hunting, to protect your house from burglaries, or to protect yourself when you're out and about all come after the right to ward off any Government threat, both foreign or domestic.

Would it surprise you if I told you I don't own a gun? I'm not a member of the NRA. I don't hunt because I buy groceries. I'd call the cops if someone was trying to break into my home. If I have a problem with someone I talk it out or run. But that's my choice and I don't choose to tell others what to do. I think people who pick their kids up from school with guns on their hip are fucking weird, insecure, and socially retarded. But I also respect their choice and would choose to not go out for drinks with them. However, I like knowing that if I wanted to, I could buy a gun today. Not after a screening period, or waiting for a permit, or getting some other kind of permission – today.

Gun ownership and the ability to buy them is a right, and not a privilege for any Government official or bureaucrat to grant. Should I have to register my purchase with a Government or bureaucracy? What business is it of theirs? Have I said or done anything to hurt another person? Why does a Government want, or need, to know who can defend themselves?

As to limiting or restricting the kinds of arms citizens can own, there is room for reasonable debate. Arms can mean anything from a knife to an F-16. A person doesn't need a tank or a bazooka to protect themselves, their property or their rights. But guns of all shapes and sizes are a proven and effective means of self-defense. If you can hold it, you can own it.

Do guns hurt people? Of course. Most of the people who die from guns are involved with, or accidentally caught in the fray of, organized crime related to drugs and prostitution. If drugs and prostitution were legal, the use of force and intimidation to monopolize the black markets for these goods and services would cease to exist. Gangs would lack the funds and influence to even try getting by on extortion. By legalizing drugs and the sex trade you'd eliminate all of the violence associated with them; criminals would be forced to either go legit or get a real job; do beer reps from Budweiser shoot it out with other beer reps from Miller? No; they compete for sales and market share of their drugs (beers/alcohol) legally.

Guns are a method of choice for the slim majority of suicides in the States; and like guns - ropes, pills, high ledges, and tailpipes aren't illegal. For all of the crimes of passion committed with guns, I suppose if there weren't guns there'd be debate over banning baseball bats and knives; the latter two of which are used as lethal weapons already.

Lastly, every time a person snaps and takes out their frustrations in life on other people with the use of gunfire, it's tragic, I know; who doesn't? But should the irrational actions of a few people justify revoking the rights of the many? Of course not. This is why we live in a democracy which can only exercise its will without infringing on individual rights and laws.

Gun ownership is a right that affords people the ability to choose whether they want to protect themselves or not. Be very wary of anyone who wants to limit or remove this right.

CORPORATIONS

They are the legal status of most businesses, which grant them certain rights and set out certain guidelines for them to follow (taxation, pay structure, laws and so on). Probably the most important function that a corporation provides a business is the sheltering of its owners from direct legal and financial liabilities; which is a good thing. For instance, if you own a store and someone slips and falls in it they can't sue you personally. Instead, they file a lawsuit against your corporation; leaving you and your private finances protected. It's fair and makes sense. However, if you did something intentionally criminal or negligent you'd be screwed personally. And that also seems fair and makes sense.

Corporations have a really bad name as of late, and with good cause. The problem with so many arguments against corporations is that people forget that corporations are only as big and successful as people choose to make them.

If you don't like big brands and big advertising, buy no-name products. If you hate a company or an industry, don't buy their shit. If a company has bad management and ruthlessly lays off thousands of people to meet bottom lines, don't work for it, don't invest in it and don't buy its products. If a company uses sweatshop labor, don't buy its products. If you know that cause marketing has little to do with helping people and everything to do with selling product, don't buy the product. If you don't like the celebrity shilling a product, don't support the celebrity's work or the product. You want more jobs in America? Let corporations pay less taxes and keep more of the money they earn. If you think there could be a better kind of business – raise the standard by building it yourself; it's a free country.

The classic charge of corporations being evil by citing examples of how companies choose to save money by making less safe products is ridiculous. It's the people who knowingly made the unsafe products who are evil. And they're stupid too; they designed a crappy product and decided to make a fast buck today at the risk of their reputation and profits tomorrow. If they were smart they'd have made a product that was a little more expensive, much safer, and have billed it as a market leader in safety to offset the perceived disadvantage of the added cost.

But don't get me wrong. Businesses and the people who run them aren't all angels. Companies have knowingly produced, or covered up after discovering, harmful products and pollution. Companies routinely commit fraud and break anti-trust laws. Unfortunately, individuals almost never face penalties. Instead the companies are fined; fined in amounts that are relative to pocket change. This creates the cost-opportunity conundrum; if the opportunity to make or save money out-totals the cost of the fine, then it's worth it to break the law. And with this, we'll now address a few major reforms that must be dealt to corporations.

THE LAW: In addition to fines, the individuals in charge of a company who knowingly sign off on or conceal practices which break the law must face personal fines and/or jail time. Moreover the fines should be at least twice the amount the illegal practice earned or saved by the corporation.

UNIONS: It should be illegal for any corporation to hinder its employees' rights to unionize. To do so is infringing on people's individual rights and their free will.

MONOPOLIES: While individuals may own a whole or part of several corporations, it should be illegal for a corporation to own other corporations. When corporations can own one another they can effectively control and limit competition. A free market can break monopolies, but monopolies shouldn't be encouraged by law.

CORPORATE PERSONHOOD: A corporation is not human. It should be given none of the rights of a human. The eyes of the law should never see it as human. Corporate personhood should be repealed with haste.

GLOBAL WARMING

How long have weathermen been recording temperatures? Wasn't there an ice age not too long ago? Isn't there a lot of evidence of extreme weather before humans started burning stuff?

The science is out - temperatures rise and fall on earth. The question is - does human activity raise it significantly on its own? The dangerous part about burning fossil fuels isn't that we're melting the planet – it's the dirty air that results and the fact that we're burning up a non-renewable resource without a viable alternative. I don't believe we are warming our planet; we're polluting it, but not warming it. But here's why it doesn't matter.

We have the technology to get off of fossil fuels. We just haven't forced ourselves to use it. Instead of creating a world bureaucracy to tax (and subsequently create profits for special interests in the process) and channel billions of dollars into corrupt Third World leaders' Swiss bank accounts... why don't we just transition out of gas and into a more powerful and renewable energy? The kind of energy that really smart people may be able to harness from the research and findings of the Hadron Collider experiment. This planet has been much colder and much hotter. Technologically advanced energy, and not bicycle lanes, is what will prolong our time here.

Take the money to be taxed/diverted away from us and put it towards such a transition of our own voluntary choosing and investment.

That was the big joke of the Copenhagen gathering – it was all about speechwriters' promises to produce less of something bad and the transfer of wealth, instead of ending the cause and source of the problem, i.e., burning fossil fuels.

If we had a world based on clean energy it wouldn't matter what side of the global warming debate you're on; the debate would be over and nature would do what it does

PRIVACY

Privacy is both a right and choice that is an integral component of free will. A free person needs privacy, as long as they aren't hurting anyone. Privacy makes a person feel safe. It starts with the right to not have people touch you in any way if you don't want them to. It's about not sharing your thoughts or personal information with others if you don't want to. And it's also about having the right to not have others around you when you don't want them around. These are the basics.

And then it gets tricky. You have to consent to a loss of privacy if you want to work in certain jobs or gain entry into certain buildings. Is it alright for your boss to monitor your web browsing at work? Seems like an invasion of privacy right? It is, but it's one you consent to for the sake of a job and to reassure your boss that you aren't playing games or watching five dudes up inside a woman, simultaneously. It's also a reasonable compromise. But your boss can't read your e-mail and you can create passwords to keep your work private. Remember, privacy is a subjective issue that requires reason and compromise to protect it and people's personal freedom.

Can an employer or Government take things from, or put things in, your body? The simple answer is that Governments can't do either. Your body is your very own private property; even if you're a criminal. A Government can, however, take your picture for documentation. If you've broken a serious law, fingerprints are necessary for proving evidence and because you've demonstrated that you may commit a crime in the future which might require fingerprints to solve the crime. But that's all the privacy a person should be ever wave to a Government.

The only thing an employer should be able to take from an employee is a cup of piss, if the employee operates machinery that has the potential to hurt themselves or others. I like to party like the next guy, but I'd like to think my pilots, subway driver, or the guy swinging the crane over the streets doesn't have a meth or coke addiction; and isn't cracked out from the previous night while on the job. The reason it's not a total invasion of privacy is because it's a reasonable safety precaution in these fields and if the employee doesn't like the policy, they can choose other work.

Of course people will say, well what's to stop Governments from requiring drug tests for everyday drivers. And I say, it's about being reasonable and doing things that are feasible.

One of the most significant parts of the Bill of Rights is this one:

Fourth Amendment – Protection from unreasonable search and seizure.
The right of the people to be secure in their persons, houses, papers, and effects, against unreasonable searches and seizures, shall not be violated, and no Warrants shall issue, but upon probable cause, supported by Oath or affirmation, and particularly describing the place to be searched, and the persons or things to be seized.

Back in the day, tyrants would oppress people by having their soldiers barge into people's homes. While in the homes they might rape a wife or a daughter or steal some food and money. They may have also issued threats against any opposition or dissent against the tyrant of the day. They might also look around the place to see what the people in it were reading, thinking, or buying, and report their findings back to the tyrant. If the tyrant didn't like what he heard, he gave the people in the home a hard go of it. He might have imposed new taxes on them, or burned something down... you get the picture. Sadly the Founders screwed up, in my opinion, with the previous amendment:

Third Amendment – Protection from quartering of troops.
No Soldier shall, in time of peace be quartered in any house, without the consent of the Owner, nor in time of war, ***but in a manner to be prescribed by law.***

They should have put a period right after WAR. As it stands now, the Government can, if it hasn't already, create a law permitting soldiers to enter your home. This is a dangerous little loophole in the Bill of Rights; although I doubt soldiers are going to be knocking on doors any time soon.

Anyway, you can see how important privacy was to the Founding Fathers and how maintaining it is essential from keeping tyrants at bay.

The ironically titled Patriot Act threw most of the Bill of Rights out the ninth storey window. In fairness, it's effective against warding off terrorists. It allows Government to screen communication and activities that it might deem as potentially threatening to the country and its citizens. But the act was drafted to be applicable to ALL AMERICAN CITIZENS.

All Americans can, if the Government sees fit, be denied "certain kinds" of free speech, protection from unreasonable search and seizures, trial by jury, being jailed without a formal charge, and protection from torture.

This act is a tool for would-be tyrants and can lead good men down the road to becoming tyrants. Being able to listen in on phone calls and read e-mails at will, throw people in jail without telling them why, toss in some jail beats and a fake drownings, prosecute people in closed-off courts, or barge into your home because they have a hunch... this is the law of the land and it's unconstitutional and totally unnecessary. Sound policing without intruding on citizens' privacy and freedom is what's needed. If you're looking for Muslim terrorists – get warrants to investigate them. Screen visa applications from people coming from countries that support terrorism. Monitor areas of warranted concern. This act, as it stands now, let's law enforcement (the soldiers of tyrants long ago) have far too many opportunities and excuses to intrude on people's lives.

The common counter to this is that if you have nothing to hide, what's the big deal? Well, if a Government can watch you, why can't you watch the Government? What's with the double standard here? It's a slippery slope. And one that always leads to people watching others, slowly telling them what they can say, do, think, wear, move, and on and on.

The Patriot Act must be rescinded and replaced with traditional and Constitutional law enforcement strategies and practices.

THE BEAST

Call it the system, the machine, the devil, Babylon, whatever – it all boils down to one thing. The system is what keeps people down and keeps them from going higher even when they're up. The system is what deprives people of their true being; consciousness in a human body ready and open to all and any experience. The system is the thing that divides people, friends, family, countries, the world. The system is the root of most of our conflicts and prevents us from resolving most of them. The system inherently fosters divides of every kind throughout humanity, our species, instead of unifying and empowering it. The system, as free as you think you are, controls us. All of us. It is the notion that we are alive to grow up, work, have friends, have kids, die, and that that's the way it is.

The system has three integral components to it: 1. Government and religion to referee the system. 2. religion/media/Government to condition our minds and actions into buying the system. And, 3. money, the oxygen and blood supply of the system.

Government, or a group of people who can dictate or impose laws that affect the daily lives of people without their say, is the ultimate form of tyranny. A Government that is representative of your views is better, but the representatives elected always seem to never do most of the things they promise; and people deserve what they get, but in our case there are few choices, if any. At the most, a Government should be responsible for defending people with a military, maintaining and organizing essential infrastructure, and providing a justice system that protects the rights of people and the law of the land.

A Government should have no say in how you live your life, spend your income, how you receive your healthcare, what you learn in school, what food or plants you consume, where and how you travel, what entertainment you consume, and so on.

Governments are formed all over the world and they separate the people of the world with their borders, money, policies, and language; and that's alright, so long as it's the will of free people. The system enables only a few thousand people worldwide to lead billions.

Religion, media, and other forms of thought control/manipulation all serve the same purpose. They condition people's attitudes towards things and life in general. They shape what you know about your world, your life, your potential. Religion teaches what it deems to be wrong and right and hinders progressive thought with laws based on books that are centuries old, derived from broken telephone word of mouth stories, translated through numerous languages, unscientific, and out of touch with the modern and developing person. Religion further divides the human spirit with which it tries to nurture by claiming superiority over other belief systems. Religions are convoluted ideological systems with contradictions that constantly contradict their contradictions: love this, kill that, do this, beat that, want this, fear that...

Media barrages people with subjective opinions, personal agendas, and other distorted perceptions of reality that, in turn, blur the media consumer's own perception of reality. Media is supported by advertising, the propaganda wing of money. Advertising often pushes false realities, consensus, and other psychological manipulations for the sake of selling things, most of which aren't essential for anything.

Money is the tool we use to measure the value of human labor, expertise, and resources. Money is earned from labor, expertise put to use, or resources sold. The more money a person earns the more labor they can have provided for them, the more expertise they can buy, and the more resources they can consume. To do anything in civilization requires money. Regardless of the supply of labor, expertise, and resources, it is money that determines the availability and access to all three; but that's the way it must be. Religions and Government (the kind of Government we have today, at least) cannot survive without other people's money. Media urges us to spend money we might not necessarily want or have to. Be aware of this.

Despite all the bullshit, we are all still free. We have choices. They may be limited to a few options, but there are always choices. Use them while not imposing them on others.

GOVERNMENT

Most kids could care less about it. I don't blame them. They don't have any real input and they can only vote for one of two balls of the same sac. But being aware of your Government and how and why it functions is important if you want to live a life with as much choice, free will and experience as possible.

Government is about the way groups of people are controlled. A Democratic Republic, the ideal Government, is one form of Government where the people control it and, in turn, themselves. It's about trying to make sure a society is accountable to the people according to laws.

An ideal Government upholds and protects the law of the land – its Constitution. An ideal Government provides a functioning justice system to resolve disputes among the people and protects its citizens' freedom and liberty. An ideal Government runs a proper justice system. An ideal Government helps to organize infrastructure. An ideal Government protects people and the rule of law with police and firefighters. An ideal Government protects its citizens by promoting and maintaining peace with other Governments, but can defend its citizens by acting with force only when attacked. An ideal Government represents the will of the people alone and has its power rooted in the electoral process of its people and the supreme law of the people. And an ideal Government protects the natural resources of the people. Anything else and the Government becomes a burden; to any and every varying degree.

The downfall of every form of Government is when it loses its purpose – to protect freedom – and instead becomes its own entity with a new purpose – to help Government, the individuals who run it, special interests that benefit from its laws, and to intervene in several areas of citizens' lives in the name of any cause.

A Government, because it is essentially the will of the people, should never be able to do or dictate to people what one person wouldn't, or would, want another doing or telling them. To this end, a healthy Government can never tell people what to wear, read, listen, to say or not say. A healthy Government doesn't control and/or own people and can't force people into service of any kind, whether it be community or military. A healthy Government can't own businesses and land. A healthy Government can't prohibit people from doing anything to their body or force them to do anything to their body, whether it is a medical procedure or the drugs of any kind they choose to consume. A healthy Government cannot tax people's labor, their income; this is an unacceptable form of pimp-like slavery. Enforced, direct income tax, comparable to forced state labor, is a principle of communism, socialism and serfdom. A healthy Government never spends more money than it has; this weakens the strength of the people by putting them in debt and putting them through the slavery of taxation to pay off the overspending. A healthy Government allows as many people, through as many different platforms, run to represent the people - all on equal footing. A healthy Government doesn't levy fines and penalties for actions that don't hurt people, but encourages and seeks out solutions that accommodate human behavior, desires, and wishes.

A healthy Government cannot be influenced on decisions with money or favors of any kind, under any pretence; the practice of lobbying (paying money to businesses or individuals who have special access to elected officials, for the purpose of influencing their decisions and financing their election campaigns in exchange) is called corruption in any second or Third World state and the same title should apply in The United States of America. A healthy Government doesn't meddle in the affairs of other Governments and doesn't rely on other Governments for prosperity; this rests the stability of the Government and the people it represents in foreign hands.

A healthy Government listens and acts in legal accordance to the will of the people. A healthy Government does not heed the will of religion or any other organized faction of people. A healthy Government always abides by the supreme laws which govern and empower it. A healthy Government never restricts the movement of its people or monitors them, when these people have not broken, or demonstrated a desire to break, any laws. A healthy Government can never infringe on the will or liberty of people to live their lives according to their beliefs, so long as the will and actions of people do not harm others or impose on someone else's freedoms and rights. A healthy Government encourages dissent, as dissent stimulates debate, thought, reason, solutions and progress.

Democracy, while not perfect, works well because it gives people a choice in what they want. A democracy that is governed by laws of reason (The Constitution and Bill of Rights) is ideal because it protects minorities from a potentially irrational and unlawful will of a majority. Democracy occurs in nature where the will of the majority prevails; tyrants are eventually killed off in the animal kingdom as they threaten the survival of species. Democracies don't wage war against other democracies, as free people with choices in life don't like fighting and dying; a free people can't be forced to fight and die.

Socialism, communism, monarchies, fascism, dictatorships and other forms of oligarchy are all philosophies of Government that limit people's ability to own land, businesses, personal income, personal beliefs, and other liberties. Instead, they divert them to, and for, the benefit of the Government with little redistribution and gross mismanagement to the people being governed.

Police and Firefighters are not Socialised. They are civil servants, accountable to and paid by us, the Government. These work sectors are essential to upholding the rule of law and the infrastructure of the land; responsibilities of Government. People's health, education, three squares a day, and savings are matters and responsibilities of individual concern.

The United States of America has an unhealthy Government. It is essentially governed by a form of socialism and fascism; and I don't say that lightly. The Government is operated by people with close ties to corporate business (through friends, family, financial supporters, or having worked for major corporate businesses before being in Government, or afterwards). Large corporate business is exerting big-time influence on our lives and the Government; this is not conducive to free-market Capitalism.

When corporate business starts dictating Government policy, which it does and is doing more so, Government becomes fascist because the will of the Government is not the will of the people, but the will of a few businessmen who use Government as a tool to meet their interests. The American Government is more and more an institution serving its own interest and the interest of the people with influence over it; instead of being an institution set in place to serve the interest of you, the general population, and upholding the laws that ensure freedom.

The trend of Government-imposed taxation, spending and regulations to "protect" and "provide" and "serve" the people is nothing less than socialism. Government is meant to allow people to protect, provide and serve themselves. Governments have always kept people behind progress, preserving the power that comes from holding Government office, penalizing productivity, and creating disincentives for productivity through social services and spending. Big Governments are behind all wars.

Governments have always been corrupt, but we're learning more about this corruption in real-time thanks to the Internet and faster global communication; some people in Government are pushing Government to censor and/or centralize the internet – our means to communicate, explore, and learn as a species. Not all people in Government are bad, but the good ones are outnumbered and largely ignored. When a Government becomes too powerful, the people become helpless and subject to the whim of Government.

It's time we move our Government towards being a more ideal and healthy one: a smaller Federal Government that the Constitution was designed and intended to produce.

POWER & CORRUPTION

Why does power corrupt? When you have power you're at the top looking down, and the people below you can't really look up. You have the ability to influence things and people with the rights or privileges of your power, your control, and if you try hard you can cover up your dishonest tracks should you misuse your power.

Power is an ego boost. It corrupts an individual by making them feel more important, more entitled and more worthy than others. And worse, it's usually difficult to question people in power; and this is an open door to the abuse of power. And so, people in power usually abuse the way they can earn money for themselves and their friends and the way they can influence things with their ideas. It's just the way most people behave in a system that breeds and affords the opportunity for such behavior to occur.

Because bias and greed through corruption are so inherent with the creation of power, positions of power should always be limited in number and in their scope. People should scrutinize any kind of power at all times before consenting to it.

POLITICAL PARTIES

They are the creations of politicians that best serve politicians and not the people they represent. Diverse ideas and debate are the necessary preconditions of healthy Government. Political parties stifle ideas and debate by offering, in the case of the U.S., one idea and two opinions with every issue of concern; instead of several ideas and several opinions. The result is narrow-minded, parochial approaches to policy. Politicians are discouraged from thinking and voting outside party lines; as such, political parties foster groupthink.

The two political parties in the United States have a monopoly on the Government. Both decide who gets the opportunity to run for office. They do this by controlling political debate. It's the favorite tactic of dictators; without debate, to put forward new and important questions and ideas for the public, the republican and democratic parties limit competition and monopolize most or part of Government power and influence. They claim that it's a fair system because you can't have any idiot running for office. And so they create minimum polling guidelines; if you don't have support of, say, 10% of the population, you can't get in the debates. But how can a candidate gain more support if they can't debate in front of a wide audience of voters? It's a rigged system.

Most of the candidates share the same ideas. The candidates seen by the party as having the most national appeal (and who will tow the party line) are given the most support from the party; it's not about integrity, it's about popularity and obtaining control. The substance of the issues debated is brutal. Candidates are hammered for minor character flaws, and their opinions on matters of personal choices that should be of no consequence to Government. Does he look confident and trustworthy? Is his wife wholesome? Is he promising to do a lot? That's the stuff that sways voters – because politicians place so much emphasis on it.

Political parties leave our democratic process susceptible to corruption. Presidents can be bought. In fact, it's now a proven fact that to win the presidency or any elected office, you have to have the most cash to pay for campaigning and advertising – the man with the biggest budget wins. But who pays for this? Public contributions help, but it's really big business that finances it all. And in return, political parties, presidents, and politicians all owe these contributors favors; favors in the form of passing legislation favorable to the business practices of these "donors." This is legalized corruption. And it leads to fascism; when business has a direct partnership and collusion with Government. In a way, the big businesses that finance our political system act like a holding company that owns the Government. This arrangement and state of affairs has been made possible thanks to corporate personhood, which enables businesses to participate in the political process, and the desire of just two political parties to retain dominance in the political sphere.

By now most Americans know, deep down, that there isn't much of difference between the republican and democratic parties. They know there is a difference between people who ascribe to, and identify with, the general ideology of each party – but they know that the parties themselves act just the same. The reason it's a Coke vs. Pepsi puppet show is because of those big business contributions.

Think of it like this: If the Godfather gave you the money to open up your restaurant, you're beholden to him and his associates. If he wants you to add or remove something from your menu, you have to. If he wants to make something that's not on the menu, you do your best to whip up something in the back for him. If he wants a discount on his bill, you make the cut for him. Why do you bend over for this guy? Because he got you where you are, you're his bitch, and if you don't oblige him he kills you. It's the same between political parties/politicians and big business; except business kills politicians by cutting off their funds or getting other politicians to vote against their initiatives. No money, no political viability. Lobbying has to go.

We can't ban political parties; you can't outlaw people's ability to assemble together with a common goal and ideology. But we can eliminate two parties from controlling debates by lowering the levels of support needed to partake in them to 5%. Doing this and eliminating Government and corporate (non-human) campaign financing would drastically clean up our elections at every level:

Every vying politician should be forced to generate their campaign finances from the actual electorate. Campaign contributions should be limited to citizens' donations not exceeding 5% of an individual's personal income. Conventions would have to be paid for by ticket sales, like a concert; which is what conventions usually amount to – entertainment. With the Internet and media, politicians have no need for tens to hundreds of millions of dollars to get their "message" out.

The remaining Government elections for different levels of office would be conducted relative to their significance. The underlying principle of 5% polling support to qualify for debating and campaign financing derived from individual, non-corporate, citizens would still apply.

I am against regulations that limit people's freedom, talent, and will; in this case limiting the money people can raise to seek office. Firstly, however, the current regulations in place serve the needs of special interest groups in society; namely, entities with large sums of money. Secondly, limiting funding for a process that isn't a part of economic productivity... isn't really limiting a person's will or ability to make a living... it's limiting a person's ability to sway voters with cash instead of substance.

The present system is a hazard to a democratic republic in that it limits the vast majority's right to options. Unrealistic and prohibitive qualifying standards for debate and multiple donations of tens upon tens of millions of dollars tip the democratic process in favor of a select few; sure everyone gets to vote, but they get to vote for one of two people who, regardless of the outcome, benefit these select few all the same.

Equal debating opportunities and democratic financial footing among political candidates is the hallmark of a free and a healthy democratic republic. The goal is to create a Government with more independents, more voices, and more ideas. Larger parties will always exert greater control over Congress, but more voices of dissent will keep them in check.

COUNTRIES

Since cave men they've been around, just in smaller forms. If a group of people within a group didn't get along, or wanted different things, they either forced the others off the land they lived on, or found new land to call their own. Wherever people have settled, it's usually because of a lack of resources or some type of conflict in the last place that drove them there. And so throughout the history of humans, people have staked out plots of land and built societies on them.

The concept of a country is a great thing in that a new one can offer people a fresh start and a reprieve from an oppressive one. A country, if it is truly free, has sovereignty which allows people to decide how they want to live. As long as there is discord between people, there will be countries; man-made comfort zones.

Countries compete against one another for resources and labor. While this is healthy in theory, it creates winners and losers. Instead of sharing technology and resources, countries, by design, create a struggle for them. It is important to note that this is a result of the leaders of countries and the systems of Government they employ; free and peaceful countries allow people to share/trade in mutual self-interest.

Countries breed nationalism which pits people against each other simply because of the place they were born. Nationalism is the propaganda wing of a country. Rooting for your country with a flag is no different than rooting for a team with its jersey; feeling a sense of pride and accomplishment in something you haven't done. Nationalism leads to arms races, soccer brawls, racism, paranoia, and other horseshit that results when people perceive themselves as separate, different, or superior to others.

A country is only better than another in its ability to afford citizens the most freedom and economic prosperity while respecting the rights of its citizens and other countries.

As long as there are several countries there will always be several obstacles to the free exchange of resources, knowledge, and the potential of people. It is up to the people in disadvantaged countries to take control of their countries and reform them emulating the foundations and principles of better, freer ones.

LANGUAGE

Arguably the most powerful tool humanity possesses is that of language, both written and oral. Language has given us the power to express our thoughts, educate ourselves, and invent. Language, or the thousands of them in existence, is also one of the most powerful things going against us. With so many different languages it's hard for everyone in the world to "get" the same message to understand each other. Language, like countries, can breed xenophobia.

The condition of humans can only improve to the extent that the people of the world can understand each other and express their minds with each other without translators and subtitles. For this reason, English should be adopted as the world's language; and it makes sense as it's the most spoken second language.

MEDIA

TV shows, Newspapers, Magazines, Radio Stations, Websites and other things that are there to inform and entertain us. Our problem isn't with how, or how well, the media informs and entertains us; there is so much content available that a person can find something to their liking. Whether certain forms of entertainment are too violent or too lascivious is a matter of personal taste and can be rectified by changing or turning a channel, page, subscription, dial, or site to something more desirable.

As to whether media bears the responsibility in part, or whole, for influencing negative behavior... there is no question that it can contribute to all kinds of behavior. But, people can read and see things and learn from them without having to replicate anything; if they have to go out and repeat what they have seen and heard, they are likely the kind of people who end up fucking up their lives, and the lives of others anyhow. They are weaker-minded people, easily influenced, with lower confidence levels; the kind of people who without the external influences would go on to do things worthy of material for writers who make up most of the stories we read and see. It's a vicious cycle.

But I'm not concerned with entertainment, or how it corrupts our youth and the mentally unstable. I don't care. I do care about how reliant we have become on news and information media; our press, the mainstream media. The mainstream media doesn't cover many important newsworthy issues. When these issues are covered, key truths, questions and facts are either overlooked or intentionally discarded. Sadly, most of us rely on the mainstream media for our information, decision-making, conversation pieces, and amusement. In a way, if an issue or event doesn't make the mainstream media, it's almost like it didn't happen and wasn't important. Likewise, the most trivial stories like celebrity infidelities often get front page coverage.

The mainstream media, which consists of a few TV stations, magazine and newspaper publishers, somehow owns the franchise on what is and can be considered credible and important news. The reason for this is the mainstream media has the money and resources to saturate the mediums our eyeballs scan on a daily basis, so much that we don't bother seeking out other sources; they are already there for us on four or five major channels, every street corner paper box, news rack, and even the software that your computer may use to lead you to a major news site every time you log out of your e-mail. Mainstream media is so pervasive you don't have to think about it.

The companies that provide you with news aren't set up and running for the virtuous notion of informing the public. A media company is a business. News networks care about high ratings. Newspapers and magazines care about high circulations and websites care about traffic. The bigger the audience, the more money that can be made off of advertisers in exchange for getting their message out to hundreds of thousands of potential buyers. Leaving our information suppliers at the mercy of business leads to just some of the following problems, all of which are unhealthy to a democracy:

1. If it bleeds it leads – this practice of emphasizing tragic and destructive events is used whenever possible because it captivates people's attention for all the wrong reasons. Death, murder, rape, crashes, fires, drowning, affairs, molestation and all of the brutal shit that can and does happen in life is not a part of daily life for most of us. It's shocking because it's not really reality and, well, there's not much we can do about it, except to try and avoid it. All of the reporting on human misfortune isn't reported on because it's of any use, but because it is so out of the ordinary to us that it attracts us; peaks our curiosity because of our fear of it. That, and we all sort of get off on tragedy, so long as it's not us. It says a lot about our culture how every night hundreds of thousands of people, if not millions, receive hot meals from volunteers and yet if a plane crashed and killed 59 people we'd be hearing about the plane for days.

2. Because media companies are dependent on advertising revenue, advertisers can influence content by threatening and/or pulling ads from media companies if/when they cover/run content that is deemed undesirable to the advertiser. To make matters worse, every major advertising agency and lobbying firm in the U.S., that matters, is owned by one of five major holding companies. These holding companies not only wield ridiculous influence, but own all of the companies that act as the voice for literally any company that matters in America. If a company, lobbying firm, or advertising agency has an issue with the material their ad's are placed next to, the guy selling the ad space is nothing but complacent to their requests to remove content.

But it's alright. Media can run the content it wishes to, just like you can consume it if you wish to. I'm one of those people who believes television and the mainstream media dumb down everything from information, entertainment, and people. What's the only solution to this dilemma?

Seek out independent news outlets a few times a week. Compare and contrast the stories, reports and opinions from the independents with those of the major media sources. Whether you do this daily, weekly, or just every once in a while – do it and you'll be better able to judge things for yourself.

Watch programs that are commercial-free. Watch more documentaries. Read more books. And when you're done consuming your media – think for yourself and don't rush to conclusions.

WAR

"I spent 33 years and four months in active military service and during that period I spent most of my time as a high-class muscle man for Big Business, for Wall Street and the bankers. In short, I was a racketeer, a gangster for capitalism. I helped make Mexico and especially Tampico safe for American oil interests in 1914. I helped make Haiti and Cuba a decent place for the National City Bank boys to collect revenues in. I helped in the raping of half a dozen Central American republics for the benefit of Wall Street. I helped purify Nicaragua for the International Banking House of Brown Brothers in 1902-1912. I brought light to the Dominican Republic for the American sugar interests in 1916. I helped make Honduras right for the American fruit companies in 1903. In China in 1927 I helped see to it that Standard Oil went on its way unmolested. Looking back on it, I might have given Al Capone a few hints. The best he could do was to operate his racket in three districts. I operated on three continents."*

– Retired U.S. Marine Major General Smedley Darlington Butler

*Please see the section on Fascism

Like a lot of gay sex in jail, war is about control. War is a way to get things by force. A nation (country) fights wars over some pretty simple shit: resources (land and the stuff on or in the land), ideology and influence (religion/politics and the stuff people believe in), as well as the money that comes with it all.

Nations can fight amongst themselves for all the reasons above in civil or revolutionary wars.

Wars way back in the day were fought over everything from hunting rights, to someone feeling insulted, someone getting raped or murdered, to the leader of a people just wanting to knock off a group of people just because he felt like it; wanted to feel and exercise that regal power over people.

WAR IS MONEY IN FIGHTING

Big time. There is money in supplying a war effort. People need to make bullets, bombs, trucks, guns, planes, food, ships, tanks, and everything an attacking or defending force needs to wage war. There are people worth fortunes today whose families owned the factories that just made the fuel pumps in planes for WWII; not the planes, the fuel pumps.

War stimulates an economy in a huge way, so much so that in a fucked up way there is an incentive to expand wars because the longer a war goes on, the more prosperous the people supplying the war effort become (it's guaranteed employment and contracts).

WAR IS AN INCENTIVE FOR MONEY

If you win a war you can claim rights to the losing country's land. With that land you can use its natural resources for trade, for manufacturing, or to set up camp to extend your economy's influence, or for your people to live on, or to get prepped to fight another war and claim even more territory/power/control.

If you fight a war to "win over a people" you can convert them to your country's way of life and get them to do business with, and even pay taxes to, your country. Hell, if all goes smoothly, they'll help you fight your next war against their neighbor.

FINANCING WAR IS MONEY

Helping other countries fight wars is an old one. If a country can weaken another country without having to actually fight it, but gains the financial alliance of the country doing the fighting, well, that's great for business. By weakening your competition you gain the ground they lose and you can extend trade with the country that did the damage.

A country can make cash and gain influence by selling armaments. The armaments can be used by an ally and the ally can defeat a common enemy. The enemy's resources can then be shared.

This is why so many powerful countries go to great lengths to make sure that the leaders of countries in the regions of their "interest" are "friendly leaders." Leaders who are ready and willing to do the bidding of the powerful nation that helps back the legitimacy of their own leadership. It's an I'll scratch your back, you suck my dick kind of arrangement that works out well for the people in control and usually screws the people of the country backed by the larger power.

WAR COSTS THE LITTLE MAN BIG MONEY

Do you really think taxes can pay for thousands of fighter jets, tanks, bombs, uniforms, aircraft carriers, food, guns, intelligence, and the billions and trillions of dollars a war costs? Governments have to print money and take on debt to cover that shit.

You, the taxpayer, pay for the war when your dollar loses its value from the printing of money and deficits, all in addition to your tax contributions. The military industrial complex, however, gets rich in the process, regardless of inflation, deficits or taxation.

ETHNIC CLEANSING

Ethnic cleansing is commonly translated to: kill off all of the people who don't believe in a specific God or who don't look like a specific kind of people. Yes it's true that such wars exist for this purpose and as a means to spread the influence and territory of a country and rid an area of an undesired cultural influence, but there is always a crucial element of economics that really helps motivate the people with the power to initiate an ethnic cleansing – money.

The people on the receiving end of an ethnic cleanse are usually poorly armed, if armed at all, and seen as a financial obstacle; they either occupy a land with valuable resources or they have a valued place in a country's economy, such as a monopoly on trade or a particular area of commerce, or they are seen as a threat to political power or national identity. For instance:

When fire was a new invention, tribes could wipe out competition during winter months simply by extinguishing the flame the other tribe depended on to light its fires for warmth and cooking; lighters weren't invented back then.

Armenians were quietly "removed" from the Ottoman Empire because of nationalism. Hitler saw this removal as a palatable precedent for his Jewish plans.

While the Jewish people in WWII Germany were seen as "dirty" they were also depicted as an economic threat.

A great deal of the slaughter you hear about in Africa is not just about religions clashing, but about a people of one religion occupying oil and/or mineral-rich land.

The natives of North America got a mouthful because they got in the way of land development and were seen, by some, as savages.

There are too many to list.

*Muslims seeking to proselytize the West, and citizens of Western nations faced with such a prospect, would be well served to read up on the various incidences of ethnic cleansing in history and their causes... to avert more tragedy in the future.

NEED A JOB?

We know that only a few people really high up in the power halls of a country can start a war (and who can avoid/prevent war). But how the fuck do they start them and how do they wage them? We'll answer the last question first.

Most countries have armies; basically people who are trained to fight other armies and have a wide array of armaments to do so. But who wants to join an army and face the prospect of death? Countries can either force citizens to join the army through drafts or mandatory enlistments, but these methods are usually reserved for when a country is losing a war, when it is involved in an unpopular war, or when a country has to enter a war suddenly.

Conscription, by the way, should also be made illegal; it rapes free will. Don't buy that you owe your country bullshit; you are owed the right to live and do what you choose. If you have to defend that right with force, you so do so by choice.

The best way to recruit soldiers for an army during peace is through incentives. In less developed countries, soldiers receive better pay and food and have power over the general population. In countries like the States soldiers can get educated, paid, travel the world, and have access to solid careers at the end of their service. The catch is that even though the perks are great, especially if you can't afford school, your life is on retainer when you sign up. Throughout history soldiers have been given better pay and higher social status as compensation for their duty.

Very importantly, Governments seek out younger men. Having less wisdom, younger men tend to not question what they are told; they take orders better and, by knowing less about life, they can be better molded, indoctrinated, and mentally and physically conditioned to carry out the role assigned to them by their authorities. Younger men have less to lose in life and are usually more willing to put themselves in danger; they're more fearless. If you do have a lot to lose in life and you voluntarily decide to put your life in danger when there is no grave threat to you or your family, well shit, you are defined as the ideal tool of war – a person who will surrender his free will to the will of others who rely on the will of others to carry out their will and objectives.

HOW ARE WARS STARTED?

So now we know how wars are waged; with the help of a country's citizenry who do the fighting for the few men who start the fights. But how do these few instigators actually start a war?

Free and rational people don't like the idea of dying a violent death; they'll only support such a scenario if they are told they have to; remember how the angry and scared emotions lead us to violence? Obviously if a country is attacked there is an immediate response from people to fight. But how does a country become an aggressor?

With the use of propaganda (like ads to get citizens to join armies) Governments can shape a country's beliefs and attitudes about another country. With the use of the media the Government can start talking about threats they perceive, or manufacture, about other countries; threats to a country's way of life or security. Countries can also start blaming their problems on other countries. Whatever the problem may be, the Government has to paint a picture of its rival as something its people can fear, hate, and want to defend themselves against.

This is done through open debate, editorials in newspapers, press briefings, television commercials, and basically getting everyone in a Government position to start talking about the negative aspects of a country, its leader, or its people. Once the leaders in Government start talking, the media starts talking, then the people watching both the people in Government and media talking, start talking amongst themselves, and then in a short period of time a lot of people get there animalistic emotions revved up and BAM – you have a real threat on your hands.

Even though the vast majority of the people who claim and believe in the claim of a threat have never thoroughly examined this threat, visited this threat, met the people who comprise the population of this threat, or understand the relationship between their country's Government and the Government of this threat. Most everyone believes in it. Why? Because people blindly trust Government, don't ask many questions and, as such, don't demand answers. Governments hedge on these weaknesses. That's how propaganda works – get a major theme – get it out in the media on repeat – condition people's views – win consent.

The substance of the propaganda can be fact or fiction (usually facts out of context coupled with fiction) just as long as it stirs up enough emotion to get people on board for a fight.

As for the justification of war there are a few.

1. You get dragged into a war out of an alliance with a country that has been attacked, and it's your obligation to help defend them. This kind of strategy locked Europe in war for hundreds of years and was the reason the Founding Fathers rejected military alliances, as you're always accountable for another country's conduct. Military alliances always lead to perpetual cycles of violence and they culminated in WWI. Avoiding alliances is responsible Government in that it assures a people of a country accountability and responsibility for its actions and it protects its people from having to lose life on account of the actions or policies of other people to whom they have no representation with. You can afford to avoid alliances and their inherent guarantee of conflict by having the best armed forces for the purpose of – defense. The whole concept of martial arts is self-defense; responsible and intelligent people are not concerned with aggression. You only knock out trouble when trouble comes knocking at your door.

2. Apropos to knocking stuff out, if you are attacked you must obviously defend yourself. This is the only time a country should go to war; self-defense. And it's the only way, up until recent years, that the United States has ever been able to go to war. The last three major wars the U.S. ever entered were because of... boats. Attack an American ship and, provided the attack was committed by another country, presto – you have a declaration of war. In WWI German submarines sank a British passenger ship (that was also loaded with munitions to be used against Germany) and killed 128 Americans – war was declared afterwards. In WWII the Japanese sought to destroy the American Pacific Naval Fleet but only found the less important ships as targets. Over 1,300 Americans were killed and war was declared. The Korean War was not an official war; under the United Nations it was dubbed police action – hilarious. The Vietnam War kicked off because the U.S. Navy attacked three North Vietnamese torpedo boats after being fired on. The next day a false report of more boat fighting led to a formal declaration of war (which makes you wonder why U.S. boats were armed and floating in Asian waters before a war anyways).

3. This relatively new concept of modern pre-emptive warfare - taking out the other guy before he can get you first – has always been referred to and agreed upon by people as a military incursion or a military invasion. It's always been illegal. You just can't go and invade a country because you think something's up, or because the country doesn't like you and they have the means to harm you. If a country directly threatens your well-being, then sure, you should defend yourself. Otherwise this doctrine, if you can call it that, is paranoid, psy-

chotic, and aggressive in the most evil nature. A country that attacks another country before the attacked country has fired a bullet, in my opinion, should be held accountable for a crime of murderous aggression. But don't be fooled, Governments taking out "threats" have ulterior motives; remember land, resources, politics, influence and money, baby; they're always the real motivating factors. The underlying factor lies in The Shadow.

With today's technology, and given ample preparation, the United States of America can destroy the military infrastructure and weaponry of every country in the world in less than a week, simply by using its air and naval forces; not the cities and countries of the world, but their respective means to wage war and/or effectively attack other countries. And so, this full-scale pre-emptive or preventative war business is unnecessary, unless your aim (like most traditional wars) is for the conquest of land or regional influence.

Unfortunately weaponry will always be needed for self-defense. But it's not so important that funding it should deprive a country of funds or run it into debt.

On a closing note I have to address all of the pro-war, pro-military people out there. For the people who think that by serving in today's armed forces they are somehow defending American values and freedoms from the threat of other nations (see bold highlighting), let me first say that you're not, and then let me say that you're destroying them. War is and always has been a way for controlling elites to use the people they control (even in a democracy where the people should be in control of themselves) to gain control over another country's elites and the people they control or represent, or both. That is the current purpose of war as far as The United States of America is concerned – control.

The Revolutionary War aside, there is only one instance in the history of The United States of America where it has waged war to preserve its freedom – WWII. The whole point of the conflict was a struggle for world domination. The driving force behind WWII was Nazi Germany and its design to gain control over Europe and then, eventually, the rest of the world. The people who helped defeat Germany and its allies were the only true heroes, patriots, and defenders of American values and freedom. There has never been before, or since, such a calculated plan for the control and domination of people.

A bunch of poorly trained, poorly armed, and poorly funded guerrilla fighters and terrorists in the Middle East, and elsewhere, while being more than capable of tormenting even the best of standing armies, is in no way a serious and grave threat to a foreign country thousands of miles away; not in the age of an armed citizenry, technology, and espionage. Could you ever see divisions of Jihadists parading through the streets of Manhattan with brigades of donkeys and beat up Toyota pickup trucks, celebrating their conquest over America, The Great Satan? Fuck no. The Nazis could have if they had rearmed after a victory over Europe. And there is no way a standing army can prevent a small group of people from delivering a bomb to a specific target worldwide; this is the business of intelligence agencies.

Lastly, going over to another land to kick some ass has some dangerous consequences. The country you think you are "defending" or "helping" always ends up with foreign bases or establishments that always try to organize its influence in the region. This policy, one of political and financial influence and gain, is the root of why America is embroiled in conflict in the Middle East and is financially insolvent (unless trillions of dollars in debt is acceptable bookkeeping). People in the military are seen by certain elements in their Government as expendable pawns to be used for procuring land, infrastructure, contracts, and maintaining crowd control.

AMERICAN FOREIGN POLICY

It's failing, goes against the ideals of the country, and is destined to lead to its failure as a country. This is so for three simple reasons. 1. Military alliance, presence and involvement in other countries. 2. Economic and Governmental influence in other countries. 3. The formation of an empire reliant on central banking and its unsound currency and economic principles.

Military alliances obligate countries to fight wars regardless of their actions. Alliances drag peaceful countries into wars they did not provoke and did not want. Military alliances ensure endless conflict by escalating the scale, i.e., the number of countries, involved in a war. Military alliances are a threat to a country's sovereignty by placing the fate of the decision to go to war in the military or political actions of another country. A country should have the means to defend itself against any and all threats, and should never rely on others for defense.

Having military bases, troops, ships, airfields, or any other kind of armed presence in another country can offend and intimidate a people and provoke them to take up conflict against you. Military presence in other countries undermines their sovereignty. Militaries are often installed to uphold political agendas and are, as such, a form of tyranny; having a military in place to maintain "order" in our country, let alone another, is the hallmark sign of despotism. A foreign military presence costs money and extends the military beyond its capacity to defend a nation properly. This results in a country going broke and its military being ineffective.

War is to be fought when a country is attacked by another country; not a group of people or rebels, but a country. War is to be fought when your life and property are under attack; not when your Government wants to implant or repel political influence. War is a last resort for the free person and the first resort of the tyrant posing as the defender of free people.

America has assassinated more leaders and propped up more dictators than any country that ever existed. The loss of life at the hands of U.S. "intelligence" agencies interfering with the political systems in other countries for economic ascendency is revolting. Manipulating entire countries and, as a result, ruining the lives of their people for the sake of a predictable political climate, trade and commerce, goes to show how hypocritical America is of its moral high ground. Overthrowing democratically elected leaders and supporting dictators are the crimes that make our Government a fucking joke and irrelevant. This is not American and it's not a reflection of Americans; it's the result of a few very powerful and foolish people. If a Government is bad for business - fuck it and move on to trade with another one.

A free country is only concerned with the freedom of its own political system and citizens. A free country trades freely and fairly with other countries; improving the lives of all citizens in the process. A free country doesn't and cannot rely on the stability of other countries to maintain its own.

If minding your own business and letting other people settle their own conflicts is "isolationism," then so be it. It's also Constitutional and grounded in reason. If people with conflicts want to trouble you with them, take comfort with the means to defend yourself. This is an important lesson for immigrants from war-torn and politically dysfunctional countries... the people who protest their Government to intervene in the affairs of their birth land; when you immigrate you leave your troubles and allegiances in the old one. The country you left couldn't provide opportunities for you and trying to involve your new country with the plight of your old one does nothing but strain and defeat the purpose of this one. If you care so much, go back. The U.S. Government shouldn't babysit its own citizens, let alone people and Governments in far-flung countries.

With its global military and economic infrastructure, influence, and dependence, America has become an empire. Empires are expensive to maintain and are prone to resentment and prolonged war. There can be no prosperity with constant war. America was conceived to escape the burden of an empire, and has become the very thing it sought freedom from. American foreign policy is failing and, like all empirical systems before it, is destined to fail if it holds its current course.

AS AN ASIDE

There is a douchebag mentality out there, the one that likes to chant "U.S.A." repeatedly. It believes America has the moral obligation to fire bullets and drop bombs to save lives and bring justice to the unjust. This, and the whole duty to spread democracy bullshit is just as reckless. Tyrants, and the states they control, are the people who go around "fixing" the things they feel need fixing. Tyrants, be they heads of state or of religion, are the people in history who went around spreading the ideals they held to be so pure and true. A lot of people died in the process.

A country, America, has the obligation and responsibility to be concerned with its own affairs. A person who is dysfunctional cannot tell or force another dysfunctional person how to act. A person that does not follow their own belief system would be insane to try imposing on, or suggesting it to others. Even when America has advanced to the state where its social conditions are improved – it does not have the right, or the obligation, to meddle with the affairs of other countries; rather, America has the right and the obligation to set an example for people in the world to aspire to.

A REMINDER TO SOLDIERS

Members of the United States Armed Forces have the responsibility to defend the Constitution. They also have the obligation to listen to the orders of the President and higher ranking officers; make sure your orders are in line with the Constitution. The Constitution was, and is, intended to protect American citizens. Never shoot or hurt a fellow citizen. Be aware of anyone who might put you in a position where you could. Fellow citizens may be a threat to a Government, but they can never harm the Constitution. Government, however, can be a threat to citizens, the Constitution and the very people entrusted to defend both.

THE MIDDLE EAST

The cradle of civilization. Land of the people who invented the alphabet. The birthplace of irrigation. The land of the people who helped progress science and mathematics. Innovative builders and traders all got their start in the Middle East. When the rest of the world was getting by on hunting, this region was a rocking hub of modernity. And then it all went to shit.

If you watch the news today it's a hub of instability. If you travel there, you'll see some brutal poverty and a lot of people struggling to get by. It's a beautiful region and so are its people. The only thing it has going for it is its rich history and the oil it has left. What it has going against it is a lack of modern social infrastructure, corrupt Government, and a poorly educated populous with restricted freedoms. Bluntly put, it's having trouble adapting to modernity.

The few people who control the wealth of the region, its oil, missed the boat on reinvesting it in the region. Investment in the form of schools and universities, capital for business, manufacturing, and technology... took the backseat to collecting lavish cars, building palaces and all of the things idiots with new money do. As a result, the elites who control the oil are rich and get to fly around the world drinking, fucking rentals, and gambling... but their region hasn't been able to foster the environment needed for people to better themselves and for business to want to invest in the region for anything other than oil.

As a result, the region doesn't have a lot of sovereignty. It's a tragic situation and one that is causing a lot of resentment. The average person on the street in the Middle East knows their land is controlled by oil interests. The Middle East is completely dependent on other parts of the world for oil exports and tourism. And all of the oil money lands in the bank accounts of a few individuals. Don't be fooled by Dubai; it's nothing more than a grand money laundering scheme that will eventually fall face first. No one is going to want to own anything there, let alone take up an office or residence, when the region becomes even more unstable.

The only hope for the region is for a secular youth to rise up and take control. Behind oil, there are three other hot button topics in the region.

.islam of advent the to prior on live to use people jewish that lands ;lands arab formerly other and ("land holy" a) Jerusalem over control people jewish gave which ,state a as Israel of formation the after off kicked only craziness The .peoples semitic both are They .religions abrahamic have cultures Both .peace relative in together lived jews and muslims years of hundreds For .result a as America begrudge and ,legs two on stand can Israel reason only the being as America see They .Israel of existence and concept the hate They .true isn't This .people jewish hate blindly muslims that believe blindly people of lot A*

.them offer to nothing has in live they land the because America into get to
trying muslims many are there that know do I .culture Western by appalled are
who muslims are there sure I'm And .*money with world the controlling as
faith jewish the of people see and Israel for support political American like
don't Other's .bombs and bullets American by killed muslims of number the
over off pissed are muslims Many .faith their of laws the against and degrading
;soil Eastern Middle on bases military has U.S. the fact the hate They .gripe
valid a is which ;oil their over control the for leaders their corrupting as States
the see Some .least at some ...Youbetcha ?America hate muslims Do

.few a of acts the of because people whole a demonize don't saying just
,demonstrated been have problems where problem a for look don't saying not
I'm .people 1,250,000,000 of group total a of part a be to claim who people
30,000 to 10,000 ,guessing liberally ,by posed risk the accessing intelligently of
instead ;with themselves associate people threatening few a religion a of because
people of group whole a fearing of trap the into fallen have world the around
people and America .mean I what know you'll and protestants and catholics
between battles the all of Think .christianity to are there as islam of interpre-
tations different many as are There .other any as define to impossible as is faith
muslim The

.jihad and fatwas the to addition in ;attempts murder and riots spark can car-
toons and books how is this of Proof .modernity with incompatible be to
proven been it's ...flaw fatal a have does ,factions religious its of account on
solely ,culture muslim the but ,cute and nice all is This .own their on problem
the resolve and out it figure to culture that within people the to up it's ,culture
a with amiss something is there If .be or ,speak ,think to what you tell people
let shouldn't you as just ;dress or ,speak ,think should they how people tell can't
You .it in people the but judge to one no for It's .is it what is culture muslim
The

.States the in pace slower slightly a at but ,Canada in here year every more this
seeing I'm .cultures or ,culture new adopt and assimilate generations younger
,time In .time is problems these resolves What .messy gets it ,well ,and Euro-
peans on values cultural their impose to wanting muslims few a with that Couple .conflict cultural a there's ;status equal them give to reluctant they're but
,diapers change and floors mop foreigners letting with cool They're .xenophobic
pretty they're ;pots melting really aren't societies European that fact the from
stem problems The .muslims immigrant with Europe in problems see We .press
bad of lot a get **They**

MUSLIMS THE

THE JEWS

All kinds of ethnicities have been persecuted in history. Most of them never endure fully intact. The Jewish people, as small in numbers that they always have been, always make it through in photo-finish fashion. What the Jewish people have in common with Muslims is that some people loudly, but a lot of people more quietly, dislike them. The Muslim antipathy is understandable given a few Muslims blowing people up. But the Jewish aversion is more complicated.

Historically Jews have been seen as Christ-killers or a people without a God; the people who killed the guy meant to save everyone. People have had distrust for them because they stick to their own, intermarry, and have never had a land of their own. Crowning themselves the chosen people pisses people off by making them feel... inferior. Being successful minorities has never helped them, even though far from every Jewish person leads a successful life; nobody likes seeing a foreigner with a funny hat and belt, do better than them. Those are the old and classic foundations of anti-semitism.

As mentioned above, the biggest problem for the Jewish people has been their relative success. Success breeds contempt. The Jewish culture stresses education and vocations that are essential. If you can perform work that everyone needs, you'll always serve a purpose. When you don't serve a purpose or have any tangible skills, you risk survival. Pursuits like carpentry, plumbing, accounting, law, sciences, entertainment and medicine are all depression-proof and in constant demand.

As a result of this cultural need to succeed, we find that the Jewish people hit way above their weight when it comes to productivity on a per capita basis. Because you can find successful Jewish people in almost every area of business, coupled with the fact that that the Jewish population is so insignificant, there are people who believe in Jewish conspiracies for control and domination. What these people fail to realize is that these would-be cabalists happen to work for, under, and with many more people who aren't Jewish. These conspiracy-minded people also fail to realize that there are several Jewish people who earn average salaries, lose their jobs, help out people of other faiths, get sick, have bills to pay, and blah, blah, blah.

ISRAEL

A group of people have done more with a useless piece of land than all the other groups of people in the area that have the advantage of sitting on top of some of the largest and most easily accessible deposits of liquid gold. It's a country and has a right to be one. And it's not going anywhere. That said, sensible people avoid the subject.

Sensible Jewish people lend their support by cutting a check and leaving it at that. Sensible Israelis and Palestinians want an end to violence, a return to the original borders, the dismantling of the wall, and to live with peaceful co-operation and commerce among one another. Sensible people don't categorize themselves by faith, culture or language; they just see everybody as people.

People lacking in sensibility don't want this. There are Muslims who believe Jewish people are living on land that is rightfully theirs by the decree of Mohammed and the man in the sky that guided him. There are Jewish people who believe that Jewish people cannot have a country until the true Messiah establishes one for them. The region is fraught with delusions and psychosis. And then we have Muslims blowing up Jews in public places and aimlessly firing rockets into villages. And then we have Jews gunning down, and blowing up Muslims in return.

Are the Israeli armed forces a human rights violator? I think they have clearly violated rights. I also think human rights violators are people who blow themselves up in, oh, a coffee shop. Both sides of the struggle for the land this nation exists on have blood on their hands.

If the Israeli armed forces have violated human rights, the issues need to be addressed in a court of law. If the Israeli armed forces have destroyed the property or lives of innocent people, the Israeli Government should provide financial compensation and prosecute the offenders.

The biggest challenge Israel faces is sustaining a viable population.

AMERICAN SOVEREIGNTY

Sovereignty is independence; the independence that enables a thing, in this case America, to choose what it wants for itself without interference of any kind from any unrelated influences, in this case – other countries or formal obligations and agreements, i.e., treaties.

As soon as a country loses its ability to control its immediate circumstances or actions in the future, it loses part, or all, of its sovereignty. Any contract or treaty that the United States enters into where the citizens of the United States have no right to vote, dissent, or alternative course of action in the matter, constitutes a breach of sovereignty.

Whenever, or should ever a situation arise where a foreign country, agency, or institution of some kind, can dictate and implement orders, rules and restrictions of any kind on The United Sates Government – the Government is effectively handing the controls over to this separate, non-elected country/agency/institution. This is a form of subordination and a loss of sovereignty. When The Unites States of America loses sovereignty, its citizens lose their stake in their lives and country.

It's for this reason that The Unites States of America must withdraw from any and every contract, treaty, agreement, or organization that diverts tax dollars or earnings of any kind from American domestic interests, limits the economic productivity of Americans in any way, or obligates the Armed Forces in any way. Do not buy into the notion the world is "interdependent" and as such concessions must be made. Do not buy into the notion that The United States of America has to be concerned and engaged with other parts of the world for its own good. This country has the obligation to have its own shit together and, should other nations want to improve their social and economic well being, be open to the trade of goods, services, and ideas with nations and people around the world. That's it. Nothing more.

FUNNY MONEY

The money that our Government and banks deal with is not theirs, has no tangible value, is created out of ink and paper, costs us money to obtain, and makes the money we do earn with real work less valuable in time through inflation (as more money is eased into the banks/money supply).

In a nutshell, money is created when the Government requests it from the Federal Reserve System. The Federal Reserve cuts the Government a check and, presto, money is created. The money created isn't real and has no value; it's just "agreed upon to be worth the amount created," and required no work or resources to come into existence. It's akin to asking your buddy, who is the banker in a game of Monopoly, to give you an extra $1000. Neither one of you did anything to generate the wealth of that $1000, but you can use it to buy property in the game. The difference in the real world though, is the money the U.S. Government receives from the Federal Reserve becomes a debt owed by the Government, or you, us, all Americans.

If that's not fucked up enough, it gets even more so. When the Federal Reserve currency (a U.S. dollar) gets circulated through the economy from, say, Government spending, it inevitably finds its way into a bank; failing that, commercial banks receive money from the Federal Reserve for the purpose of providing private loans, or a bank gets money from citizens in the form of deposits/savings. The laws of the banking world state that for **every dollar** a bank holds as a deposit it **can create** and lend out **nine**. The bank did and does nothing to give this money value, but it can turn it into even more money on its books for the purpose of lending it out as loans; the overwhelming majority of money it lends out and manages doesn't even exist in physical form as paper bills – it's all represented as numbers in computers, and was represented in accounting books before the advent of computers. And the bank makes money off of this money created by the "one dollar can be used to make nine more" principle, in the form of interest - interest that individuals and businesses have to pay with real money derived from actual work and profit.

To really understand how warped this whole concept is, look at it like this: all of the interest you pay on your mortgage and business or personal loans to the bank... the bank earned that profit out of thin air... doing nothing... creating and giving you that cash based on the smaller sums of money stored in their accounts. Why should you be grateful for the loan(s) when the bank did nothing for the money it lent to you, and then taxes you on your hard work for the so-called opportunity/privilege of the loan(s)? The small amount of interest you earn from saving your money in a bank is nothing compared to the interest the bank can earn off of it when it takes your savings, turns it into more money and then charges higher interests rates on it through loans.

The Federal Reserve also creates unstable business cycles by controlling the interest rates at which money is loaned. When the rates drop, people borrow more. When the rate increases, people borrow less and have to pay more on the money they borrow. It's an unstable practice that creates booms and busts of all sizes.

~

This system was created by bankers, for bankers; no conspiracies, no bullshit, just a chilling fact. The Federal Reserve is a system that helps banks, but hurts the U.S. Government in the long run.

It helps banks because 1. They get cash that doesn't cost anything 2. If they go bust it doesn't matter because they never invested in anything in the first place and every dollar they made was gravy profit, and 3. If they go bust they can always go to the Government for more liquid, worthless cash in the form of bailouts (a practice that has been going on for decades).

The system helps the U.S. Government in that it can go the Federal Reserve and get more cash to pay for the shit it wants, but can't afford; it's like a credit card and the taxpayer bears the brunt of the debt and interest. Socialism can't exist without a central bank; taxes can't cover the spending of a socialist system, but a virtual printing press, or "quantative easing," can.

It hurts the U.S. Government by decreasing the value of its currency through inflation and, in turn, erodes its citizens' personal wealth and the country's sovereignty (when both can't afford to stand on their own two feet and borrowing is required to keep afloat)

If we are to restore this country's economic soundness, we need to deep-six the Federal Reserve System and bring back honest, sustainable banking practices and a money supply that is backed by a tangible commodity.

Gold and other precious metals are scarce, useful, and have a value that we can all agree on. Pieces of paper share none of these qualities. If so, why do we place our trust and money in something created by a glorified photocopier?

Having dollars that represented a value of precious metals would make our earnings safer, our economy more stable, and our Government more responsible and honest.

COMMUNISM

I get it. The aim of communism is to create a state that is egalitarian and devoid of social stratification. The Government controls the means of production and the people receive what they need. The philosophy is intended to do away with the exploitation of workers with the use of force, instead of free will and choice. Property and possessions aren't owned, they are shared. The Government controls the system and everyone's "needs" are met while the people in Government are free to pursue their wants.

It doesn't work because people's needs, desires, talents and choices aren't the same. With communism, everything is done for the sake of the state, with the individual coming second. In attempting to help individuals, it crushes them. Individuals are not common.

I have yet to meet a professional, a stripper, a construction worker, a store owner, or an artist who lived under communist rule who has a good thing to say about it.

SOCIALISM

"Give a man a fish, and he'll eat for a day. Teach a man how to fish, and he'll eat for a lifetime."

It's similar to communism in that the state owns the businesses and regulates production and supply. The Government can be democratic and you can even own land. Like communism, it's about creating a more equal society by means of Government intervention. But it never works out that way; it is a philosophy and form of governance that is incompatible with liberty. The system cramps people, because people, while equal, have different desires in life. Some people want to work more than others. Some people want to consume things more than others. Some people have more talent. Some people are more responsible. Some people can offer things for less.

Socialism lives in the dream world of equal and shared services for all, failing to understand that the means for these services has to come from making laws to eliminate competition and that divert money from somewhere; namely, other people's ability to work and produce and their bank accounts and paychecks.

People with nothing in a socialist system love it. They see the rich or comfortable as deserving to have to pay for the things they use; even though everyone else who pays taxes shoulders a burden for their benefit. In the process they lose their independence to the state, penalize productivity, and leave others paying more for things inefficiently, that they may, or may not, use and want.

Socialists are of the mindset that they can deem when a person has enough money and when they should be forced to spend it on others. Socialists believe this mind-set is moral. I believe it is a mind-set that is irrational, arrogant, parasitic, lazy, envious and immoral on the grounds of its criminal foundation – the involuntary diversion of money from people. There are socialists who believe people should pay 40%, 60%, even 90% of their income to fund the wants and needs of other people; the wants and needs that healthy individuals have an obligation and responsibility to provide themselves with for the sake of self-reliance and this thing called... dignity.

Socialists believe your earnings aren't your exclusive right and property... in essence, they believe your earnings are a privilege to be shared. To use a classic and brutally blunt example, they think a person should be grateful to keep half the loaf of bread they made, because half a loaf can make a sandwich.

And of course, socialists claim that everything is a right; failing to realize, or recognize, that rights (things like free speech and a raft of other freedoms) don't cost anything. Goods and services, however, do cost something. While you have a right to medical treatment, you do not have the right to have it for free. You have a right to own land, but you do not have a right to have it given to you. You have the right to read books, but you do not have the right to have them bought for you. You have the right to attend Harvard, but you do not have the right to have your tuition comped. Is this getting annoying yet?

When you start touting that a person shouldn't have to pay for goods and services in this life, or that someone else should work and pay for things for them... well, if you can't see the dilemma this philosophy has built into it... the part of your brain that should be sounding off with logic and reason has been replaced with a dial tone.

DOES AMERICA HAVE A HISTORY OF SOCIALISM?

Socialism really took hold in the States during the Depression of the 1930s. Before that, the States was the bedrock against it; a place that put the welfare of the group in the hands of individuals. The Federal Reserve System and Government intervention in the economy created what we all now call a bubble in the market. Not a bubble that occurs in natural free markets, but a bubble created by manipulating inflation, business regulations and business practices. People panicked during a stock market crash (that the Federal Reserve was intended to prevent) and lost money when the banks couldn't pay their depositors. With people broke (although most did get the majority of their money back from banks), businesses failed and unemployment spiked to dangerous levels. To make matters worse, farmers suffered through extensive droughts; even before global warming. Things were a mess.

In a situation like this, much like today, the first thing that needs to happen is fast access to sound capital. People still need to live. And people need to run businesses to provide goods and services – and pay for the employees to provide them. Bad businesses should have been left to fold, leaving a void for new ones to replace them. The new businesses would have provided the goods and services that were in demand, instead of producing things just for the sake of giving people things to do. Gradually, the market, jobs, and wealth would have returned to the system. Soup kitchens, shelters, the Salvation Army, and the like could have helped in the transition process. It would have been temporary and would have saved the nation from continued instability down the road. Believe it or not, Darwinism can and should be applied to economics.

Instead, Big Brother stepped in to save the day with the New Deal, or Government economic planning. The deal replaced the notion of private, free-enterprise solving problems, and replaced it with the socialist notion that a Government should act as an enterprise in and of itself; allocating and managing employment, business, and social aid where it best sees fit. To people with nothing in a restricted free-market environment (the exact kind of environment that spawns dictatorships, socialism, and communism) it was like awaking to a dream come true. A chance at a Government funded job and/or a "free" check in the mail.

The New Deal used money, created out of debt and massive taxation, to finance elaborate infrastructure and financial stimulus projects. The concept was simple. Give people something to do, like build a bridge or road, give them a check, and then they stimulate the economy by spending the check and paying taxes. The Government even got into the business of price fixing and dictating labor costs/wages. There are books written on how the New Deal disrupted what was left of the free market after the adoption of The Federal Reserve. Read them if you'd like.

Did it work? Nope. It created a pile of debt, unaffordable entitlement, and did anything but create a sustainable economy with a large middle class. What got America out of an economic depression wasn't Government spending. It was war; a real and needed mobilization of capital and production. The New Deal was the same kind of socialist economic planning used by another Government. National Socialism in Germany got the economy and war machine going at the same time as the New Deal using similar tactics. Hitler had a whole series of state-subsidized infrastructure and manufacturing projects initiated for the war effort and the rebuilding of the economy.

The problem with the New Deal, and socialism in general, is that it failed to factor in sustainability, personal choices, free market principles, and the Constitution. It's nice to give people jobs, build infrastructure, and give people money. But economic planning is financed through debt and taxing people's trade, purchases and income with force – the threat of imprisonment and asset seizures. Is this the land of the free or the land of the people who work under and for the Government?

Another problem with the New Deal is that it created entitlements; people grew dependent on, and expected, Government assistance. This creates a disincentive to be productive and prudent with personal choices and finances. Lastly, because the New Deal created debt and set a precedent for the expansion of costly Government, people will perpetually have to sacrifice more of their hard-earned money to support Government spending. The less money people have to show for their work, the less freedom and choices they have, the less money that can flow through the economy, and the more of an influence the Government has over the lives of everyone. And the more spending that can't be paid for through taxes has to come from borrowing and printing money; which leads to more debt and less sovereignty.

And we're seeing it get worse. All in the name of "helping people" who should be helping themselves.

FASCISM

A form of governance and economic philosophy that is almost always associated with right wing politics. Fascism is actually a left wing philosophy on account of its dependence on Government. Call it fascism or corporatism if you'd like to be polite... it's a system of private business using Government to further private business practices. Instead of Governments owning or controlling private business, as is the case with socialism, with fascism we get private business literally controlling Government; to form and protect monopolies by stifling competition through unbalanced treaties, taxes, regulation, grants, permits, trials, legislation, you name it. Whenever a business can get Government to overlook or pass a law that guarantees it a profit, instead of earning that profit on a free market, fascism is present.

I can't tell the people who bash "Capitalism" enough that what we are seeing so much of today isn't the brutal effects of Capitalism, but a mix of socialism, fascism and individuals knowingly committing crimes. To say that Capitalism is wrong is like looking at a prison and saying that humanity is wrong. Most people are honest and decent; some people use their freedom of choice to destructive ends... maybe this is an unpopular notion, but I don't believe that these people and their poor choices should fuck up everyone else's ability to make choices in life... and that the actions of lawbreakers make choices in life wrong.

It's fascist practices and environments that allow and encourage real economic mischief and the ensuing damage. True Capitalist markets repel profiteering and monopolies. Governments are the agent that allow these things to occur by making them legal; the same agent that is suppose to establish and enforce laws to prevent them.

CAPITALISM

Liberty

1. Freedom from arbitrary or despotic government or control.
2. Freedom from external or foreign rule; independence.
3. Freedom from control, interference, obligation, restriction, hampering conditions, etc.; power or right of doing, thinking, speaking, etc., according to choice.

Capitalism is just a word for "the ability to work, buy and sell things for the best compensation and price you can find."

It's the system of choice and freedom. If you have a problem with business practices within a Capitalist system, don't blame the system, blame the people. It's about letting people produce and subsist by the free production and exchange of goods and ideas. Instead of the Government owning the means to produce and distribute a product, people do so on their own. The result is more choice for the consumer and lower prices as companies and individuals strive to attract business. You're free to work where you want and buy what you want. If you're not happy with the work you do or what you can purchase, you're free to improve your skills and get a better job, start your own business, and shop somewhere else. Hate the system altogether? You're free to move up north and live off the land or any other way you see fit.

If employers pay high wages and provide extensive benefit programs (benefits which can be considered wages as they are commodities worth cash out of pocket), awesome; the worker is afforded the means to acquire not only what they need, but what they want, and still has entrepreneurial freedom if they so choose. This is ideal Capitalism. If an employer pays a low wage and offers no benefits... find a better employer or acquire something that makes you more appealing to better, higher paying employers. Or work for yourself.

Problems arise when the Capitalist system, through monopoly, resembles a socialist economy. You get a few companies controlling all of the means of production or resources, which stifles competition and healthy markets. So do we impose regulations and other controls on business to "level the playing field?" No. The market corrects itself; a more innovative company is allowed to enter the market and offer a better price, thereby toppling the monopoly. More competition equals lower prices.

Don't like big banks and oil? Put your money in a credit union, drive a solar-powered car, and invest in this "green" movement. Better yet, make a better bank, car, and means to get off of conventional energy. If a law prohibits you from making a product like, say, hemp fuel – do not say "well that's Capitalism protecting oil companies." It's not. It's Government protecting oil company monopolies; a far cry from Capitalism.

As just touched on, a serious problem is that the free market system isn't really that free today. Larger and larger corporations are developing an anti-capitalist mentality to ward off competition. They are using Government to manipulate laws to their advantage. It's a strange sort of fascism and bigger Government will only make things worse. A free market and politicians kept in Constitutional line will correct this. Until such a change takes place, corporations will maintain and create monopolies that can't be broken.

Private enterprise takes a deservedly bad reputation whenever businesses move into socialized countries and buy public resources; the companies go on to charge dramatically increased prices for things like water and food only because they are allowed to monopolize with Government consent.

Access to capital is tight. Businesses that should fail because they are shitty businesses are propped up by socialist measures in the form of bailouts. In a free market, where there is unsound management or a lack of demand, the market (consumer) forces prevail and a better business fills the void if the demand is still there.

Central banking manipulates the Capitalist free market by interfering with interest rates (which determine access to capital/loans) and, as a result, keeps individuals and businesses from saving and producing their own independent capital. When interest rates are arbitrarily hiked, people have a hard time making higher payments.

A handful of holding companies own thousands of companies, which is quasi-monopolistic. And businesses aren't putting enough wealth back into the system on account of foreign labor and foreign manufacturing.

There is a socialist mentality prevailing in places, which sees the unethical collusion between business and Government as "Greedy Capitalism." This reveals true ignorance; it's not greed, it's fascism. Capitalism isn't getting away with murder – it's being murdered.

Is Capitalism responsible for all of the wars? No. Free countries, or people, trade freely with one another. Are "free countries" in the world traded with on unfair terms? Yes and no. Yes, in that there are countries that sell their goods and services at prices astronomically lower than we would be accustomed to. No, in that the initial lower return on resources and labor eventually strengthens these countries to the point where they raise their standards and become able to earn more on their goods and services. Wars that are waged for land and resources are not a product of Capitalism. They are a product of people who want to steal and manipulate land and resources unfairly. Please do not blame the system, blame the negative actions of people. If the whole world was run by either communist or socialist systems, do you really think war would end? Of course not. Only when the world is a place for people to think, live and trade freely will major wars end.

Lastly, land ownership and the ability to choose where and what to buy and sell are essential components of freedom. Communism seeks to outright abolish these principles and socialism limits them.

THE WELFARE STATE

Don't ask what your country can do for you. Don't even ask what you can do for your country. You can get more for yourself and do more for your country when you ask and do more of yourself.

The principle of a welfare state is that a Government can help people better than they can help themselves; that a Government can manage money and services more effectively than individuals. The belief is that everyone should have access to necessities in life. The problem is the necessities of life cost money. The Welfare State's solution is to try and pay for everything through taxes. It doesn't work; proof is how shot to shit America is right now. When it does work, it costs people a lot of money and doesn't work for long. And it's socialism – limiting people's purchasing power (which is tantamount to freedom) for the sake of state-controlled services that may or may not be wanted by the people who involuntarily pay for them.

The United States of America has become a country that gives people services and entitlements that they would be better off acquiring themselves, if they wanted them. Its Government provides these services in ways that are harmful to the stability of Capitalism and free markets, personal freedoms, liberty and the very soundness of the Government itself. It's all because taxpayers waste their money giving it to their Government, which then manages and redistributes the money in wasteful ways through its "Programs and Agencies." This is done all in the name of helping people. It should be made clear that people don't give their money to their Government – they are required to by the laws they allow their Government to create and impose.

In the process of giving money to their Government, people become less wealthy and the Government racks up debt to pay for what it can't provide with tax revenue. The end result is a huge Government that does much more than just represent the people and enforce the law - it actually becomes involved in every facet of their lives – and we see a bunch of people lose their independence by becoming reliant on the Government to pay for and provide them with things they should be overseeing themselves. People still have a hard time understanding that the necessities of life are more affordable and reliable if they can be pursued in a competitive free market, with the freedom to choose how to spend their money.

BUREAUCRACY

You have to remember that people solve problems. Governments don't solve problems. Governments can only uphold laws and preserve the freedoms required for people to solve problems on their own. Bureaucracies are mini-governments that Governments form in an attempt to manage people's affairs. Bureaucracies are effective in dealing with areas of society that require legal and regulatory oversight, but that don't involve a lot of personal choices. Dealing with driver's licenses or parking tickets requires an organized structure to ensure order, accountability and efficiency. Bureaucracies are great for that shit. Frustrating at times, but they work. They set up guidelines and procedures that people follow to get a standard result.

Problems arise when bureaucracies are put in place to oversee things in our life that we can manage ourselves. Bureaucracies for fishing permits, liquor licenses, construction permits, vehicle registrations and every other license, permit, form and piece of paper you can think of, now preside over almost anything we can do and own. Red tape limits our freedoms, complicates matters, and slows progress. All in the name of helping us. Did you ask for any of this help?

Bureaucracies aren't effective because they can't adapt to changes and the wide range of human circumstances. The way they dictate guidelines interferes with our choices. When bureaucracies face new problems they don't resolve things with innovative efficiencies – they get bigger. They make more rules for people to follow and create more paperwork and fewer options.

It costs us money to move through bureaucracies by paying for all of the necessary licenses and permits and it costs us money to pay for the actual running of the bureaucracies themselves. Every bureaucracy has to pay for rent, desks, computers, phones, photocopiers, pens, chairs, computers – you name it. Every bureaucracy has to pay for staff and their benefits and pensions. But it's not the bureaucracies that pay for this stuff – it's you.

The quick fix is eliminating any bureaucracy that isn't directly related to the functionality of federal, state and local Governments. If we want to have a realistic and plausible change in Government and a tangible shift away from the Welfare State we have, there are two Government programs that could be dissolved relatively soon; before they bring the house down, as they will in a generation, or less.

SOCIAL SECURITY

The premise of Social Security is that people aren't responsible and smart enough to manage their savings for retirement. Because of this assumption, the Government takes it upon itself to tax employers and employees, a bit over 12% a year, and use the funds to send a check, averaging about $1,300 a month, to retirees, people with disabilities, widowers, and children. Talk about a shitty return on your investment.

Taking people's money to manage their retirement for them is forced financial planning. It's wasteful, creates dependency, doesn't even afford people the money they need to live comfortably, can't keep pace with increased costs of living and a devaluing dollar, and isn't sustainable as people live longer lives and receive payments for all those medically-extended years of life. The biggest joke of all is that the Government dips into the money it collects for Social Security and uses it for spending on other things. Additionally, if the Government cannot meet the financial obligations of Social Security, it covers the difference by either taking on debt or raising taxes.

We can end it by discontinuing Social Security for those who have yet to pay into it for more than five years, and simply reimburse them over a period of time. Let the younger generations free up their money and independence to save and invest as they see fit. Let those who are older continue to contribute and "benefit," but phase the program out within a specified time frame.

HEALTHCARE

Is it a right? No. It's a service, with rights built into it. It's not a right just like clothing, three meals a day, a house, a spouse and good health are all not a right. Rights in life don't cost money. Rights are ideas that are essential for freedom. Rights might cost effort to preserve or money to fund the effort needed to preserve them. But rights are priceless. Anything else needed to live life, as life is a struggle for survival, comes at a tangible cost. It's our rights that enable us to better pursue our needs and wants in life.

Universal healthcare (socialized medicine) would be amazing. So would universal vacations and groceries. The problem is healthcare, like vacations and groceries and any want or need you can think of, costs money. People have to pay for it. The cost of universal healthcare (socialized medicine) always increases on account of inflation, population growth, unnecessary appointments, mountains of bureaucratic paperwork and management, and old people who just won't die (the operations they have and medicines they use cost a shitload to keep them alive a few extra years). To pay for universal healthcare (socialized medicine), Government has to take money from people.

Seeing a doctor in Canada isn't a big deal. You go, wait, and in most provinces the doctor charges the Government (taxpayer) for the visit. In Ontario our sales tax is 13% (down recently from 14%) and our combined provincial and federal income tax rate ranges from 21% (the $37,000-$40,000 earners) to 31% (the $41,000-$81,000 earners) and 40% and up for those who make more. Add that to huge property taxes and you're working 3 – 6 months for the Government. But, hey, if you have a heart attack, at least you'll get surgery if the ambulance (which isn't completely paid for by taxes) gets you to the operating room in time.

The Canadian system works if you're about to die or you are suffering from a terminal illness. Waiting times and schedules are so ridiculous now that people, who can afford to, go to private clinics for prompt and full treatment. In the Golden Horseshoe, a densely populated area around the western part of Lake Ontario, a lot of people don't even think twice about driving to Buffalo for MRIs and other services/procedures that have a waiting list, if they can. For people with relatives or friends who are doctors in Ontario... it is quite common for them to get bumped in line at hospitals for screenings and procedures and save the 3-12 month waiting lines, or the drive to a Buffalo hospital. That's right, people living in a First World country have to use connections to get screened and operated on in a timely fashion.

The system does treat everyone eventually, but it's failing as all systems that are used by people who don't pay for it directly do. Our population is growing and ageing. More kids in need of checkups and more seniors undergoing multiple surgeries and taking expensive drugs means more money that has to be diverted towards the system. There is a limit to how much of other people's money you can come up with. The bureaucracy that oversees our healthcare is hopelessly over-managed and uses a profligate amount of tax dollars just to organize... health records. Patients abuse the system by seeing doctors when they don't really have to. And I'm sure, but can't back it up, that doctors abuse the system by booking unnecessary appointments and overbilling.

Doctors are capped on how much they can earn. That's right, the Government in Canada sets limits on what doctors can earn. The billing caps are in place because there isn't enough money in the system. It hurts the country because a lot of good doctors go to the States where they are free to earn what they can get and what they deserve. Personally, if you can save or repair a life just once, I think you're worth a credit card with no limit and no payments for life. In the end, we have huge taxes to justify a huge system that doesn't work efficiently and racks up debt. And it doesn't even cover dental.

What's alarming though, is that Canadians don't pay for medical insurance. Americans think they are getting socialized medicine, but many people will still have to purchase insurance by law. The whole point of Government medicine is that you don't pay directly out of pocket for anything. And yet many Americans will be required to hold some kind of insurance or face fines; if you read the part on fascism, you'll be as shocked about this as I am. You can force people to have driving insurance because they are partaking in a privileged, non-essential, activity that can cause harm to others. Your health, however, can't be chosen to be lived one day or the next and can't be a liability to anyone else, save for family members. To make people buy a product or service from a company with the force of law is... fascist.

So for all of the Americans who think their Government can organize and run an affordable healthcare plan – sorry, it's not possible. You're going to pay a shitload of taxes for a watered down version of socialized medicine. Proof is how insolvent Medicare and Medicaid both are. The country is trillions in debt, and counting quickly, and people want to add a trillion-and-counting dollar program that won't even cover everyone. Still think Government can solve economic and business decisions?

Before we can look at a possible solution, we need to identify a major problem with U.S. healthcare. The medicine and service is state of the art. But the cost for it is absurd. I'd like to know how spending two nights in a hospital to have a baby costs between $5,000-$10,000. Two nights in a suite at a luxurious hotel, with lobsters, porterhouses, call girls, champagne and an eight-ball on every table in the room costs less than that. I'd like to know why a lot of people with insurance end up spending a couple of grand out of pocket to have a baby? This is insane and it's just one area of medicine. I remember I had to have an x-ray on my shoulder once. A few lousy x-rays cost me over $600. Six-hundred dollars to say "ok, you're fine, just give it some rest for a couple of weeks." Maybe I have an entitlement issue, but the tab seemed really steep. Would I have been better off having a Government foot the bill?

It woke me up to the reality that the States needs more healthcare competition. Just like car repair shops compete with brake specials, we need hospitals and doctors who compete with checkup and x-ray specials. I'm not kidding.

The middle-men aren't the answer. HMOs and insurance companies are massive businesses. Massive because they make money not on selling wants and materialism, but providing access to essential needs. There are actually three things that are certain in life – death, taxes, and requiring medical attention. These massive businesses jack up the cost of healthcare in mind-blowing ways. Advertising, lobbying, staffing, paperwork and the need to pay shareholders, make these businesses increase the cost of what it is they sell – access to doctors, hospitals, treatment, and drugs. What's worse is that these companies routinely preclude people from choosing the treatments and doctors they can have because of the rates and procedures they negotiate with allied hospitals and doctors in an effort to cut costs.

I'm not against people making a profit, but people are entitled to the best their money can buy; nobody pays for insurance to get the least expensive treatment. These two institutions don't help you get better or offer you security; they are an obstacle and financial middleman in the way to your treatment. They should be used as a last resort.

So do we limit business? Do we create regulations? Nope. We use our ability to choose. We could force healthcare providers like doctors and hospitals to lower their costs by being self-reliant; by choosing our medical care as we see fit and paying for the best deal ourselves on the free market. How do we do this?

It starts with small and large businesses creating healthcare funds much like 401k funds. A healthy, diversified mutual fund is a solid long-term investment. A mutual fund or 401k tied to one company leads to disasters like the spoiled retirements of workers who were banking on a little known company with a big "E" on its stationery. If workers were able to invest in a healthcare fund, matched by their employer, a miracle would happen. Everyone invested in the fund would be able to, in time, take from the fund what they needed to pay their medical expenses. If you were laid off, fired, or decided to retire, you could take your rightful share of the fund with you; in fact if you retired you'd have to. The fund would have to be exempt from taxes and would even yield more returns if we had a proper currency with next to zero, or just zero, inflation.

To get the fund started and mature enough to the point where it could be used to pay for healthcare, workers and employers would purchase temporary health insurance. Once the fund became mature enough to cover medical expenses, workers and employees would be able to drop their insurance and become self-reliant on the fund. Businesses and employees would have to be legally prohibited from using any fund money for business or personal expenses. Employees, however, would be able to use their share as they see fit in the event of unemployment or retirement. And if the business went tits up, all of the money in the fund would be distributed proportionately to the employees.

If this doesn't appeal to business or employees, they should be free to access any insurance company they'd like, and pay for it with their own money. As for taking care of the less fortunate, do we just let them die or suffer on the street? Can you show me one hospital in America that has kicked a broke or uninsured patient out on the street to die? For every person who is forced to consider which appendage they'd like to save... did they ever consider going to another, more honest, doctor? Most reasonable doctors will treat patients who are in serious trouble. For those people who cannot afford healthcare the choices are simple – go to charity-based hospitals. I'm sure there are doctors willing to see one or two uninsured patients a day, or who would take a small amount of cash to pay for a routine visit. It's about being reasonable.

If we didn't have income tax, companies lobbying politicians for favorable business regulations, and we had doctors and hospitals competing more to lower costs, more people could take healthcare into their own hands. Insurers actually covering expenses and not doing everything in their legal power to reject claims would also be a great help. Do this and we'd be healthier, freer, less indebted, and off the socialist path to ruination.

REMEMBER

The problem is that citizens, that is to say taxpayers, love Government spending – they think it's free shit - without understanding how wasteful it is to let second and third and fourth hand parties spend their money for them. They don't understand that they'd be better off saving and spending their money on their own terms based on their own informed choices and needs.

REGULATION

Liberty

1. Freedom from arbitrary or despotic government or control.
2. Freedom from external or foreign rule; independence.
3. Freedom from control, interference, obligation, restriction, hampering conditions, etc.; power or right of doing, thinking, speaking, etc., according to choice.

There are people who don't feel safe doing things, putting things in or on their bodies, or using things that haven't been deemed "safe" by Government. Instead of consuming things from reputable sources and based on sound information, yes, there are people who need a bunch of people paid by tax dollars to tell them it's alright to eat this, swallow that, and sit in those. These are the same people who believe we need laws for everything. Laws to stop this and help that. It's a mentality that's based on having others conform to arbitrary desires using the force of law; instead of the force of logic, reason and personal choice.

Federal agencies that oversee the safety of consumer goods do serve a valuable purpose. They ensure things are safe. They do this at an exorbitant cost to taxpayers, while people still get hurt and businesses and consumers are burdened with additional costs.

The Food and Drug Administration now costs Americans $3 billion dollars a year. A few billion dollars to test and approve the food* and drugs on the market, biologics evaluation and research, testing radiological devices, and funding for veterinary medicine. The result is that people still get sick and/or die from food and prescription medicine. Many more people die or get sicker when perfectly good medicine doesn't hit the market when it should on account of FDA testing delays. Are we better off with the FDA? No.

It may come as a surprise to you, but, believe it or not, food suppliers and pharmaceutical companies don't want to hurt or kill people with their products; even if they can make a quick buck in the process. If they do intentionally hurt people they can be punished by law and people can end up broke and in jail. They both want to stay in business and the quality of their products is the bedrock of their respective brands. How do they stay on top of their shit? Self-regulation based on standards set by law**; standards agreed to by the scientific community then made law by legislators. Companies use their own staff and technology to ensure product safety and thereby maintain the good standing of their brand and products. Self-regulation deservedly gets a bad reputation from the financial industry because many areas of the financial industry, such as derivatives, are off the books to anyone, let alone a regulatory agency, who wants to analyse them; this is the exact opposite of a "free" and "open" market. But the laws to punish individuals in the financial sector for illegal or negligent incidents are strong and effective.

In addition to self-regulation, private product reviews and safety digests are an effective means of informing consumers about the goods they buy. A bad review of a car's braking system or the conditions of a plant where food is canned can devastate a business much more than a code infraction issued by a Government agent.

Case in point, what would be more efficient? Buying a Zagat guide that rated the quality and cleanliness of a restaurant based on editorial reviews and customer feedback, or having a Government bureaucracy put in place to do the same thing? One costs taxpayers nothing, doesn't threaten business with scarlet letter window signs of Government failure, yet compels them to be sanitary, and can be paid for through the sale of a useful guide. The other costs taxpayers money, fines businesses that haven't hurt anyone, and forces them to have a clean kitchen once a year for inspection.

It comes down to common sense. If business can't hide information that is essential to making informed decisions, under the guise of personal privacy rights, people can govern and regulate themselves. The amount of regulatory red tape that a person or business needs to wade and slash through today cripples and punishes progress. When an issue of real concern can't be reconciled between people, or if a law is broken or someone gets hurt, you take it to the courts. It's pretty simple and it's the way our society was intended to function from its inception.

* The Department of Agriculture also inspects food. It also provides nutritional assistance to children, subsidizes crops, markets food, maintains forests, and does many more things people can and should do for themselves and their interests. In 2008 the USDA had a mandatory spending budget of $67 Billion. In 2009 it was $96 Billion. In 2010 it was $108 Billion. $123 Billion is slated for 2011, up 84% from just 2008. Will Agriculture see an 84% expansion or improvement in 2011 from 2008? Am I the only one laughing at this?

** Our legal system is the largest regulator in place, as it should be. If laws and contracts are broken, the people and businesses that break them are accountable to the courts. Jail time and crippling fines (not fines that can be absorbed by business as an expense, but the kind of fines that make a man contemplate sucking a dick for reprieve) are the surest way to keep goods and services safe. This is why a society's justice system, above even its economy, is so revealing of its condition.

TAX

My language here might sound extreme, but its veracity is indisputable. Tax is money diverted from individuals to pay for the support of something that may or may not be of benefit to them directly or indirectly.

Taxation, the ability to legally divert money from people, is in simple terms – wrong, illegal, and a form of theft. No one has the right to take the money that you earned with your time, effort and ingenuity – involuntarily; no one. Every extra penny you have to spend on an item above the sale price is a form of extortion. Every penny your business has to pay from its profits to a second party collector is a form of extortion. Every penny you have to divert from your paycheck to a collector is a form of extortion; a nicer, more decent kind of slavery. Even in the land of the free if, in your pursuit of life, liberty and happiness, you don't pay your taxes... you go to jail.

The reason people consent to taxes is pretty simple. We entrust our Government to maintain our civilization. With taxes we get a military to defend us, a justice system to prosecute criminals and enforce matters of law, politicians to oversee governance, and police and firefighters. This is all a free people should want their Government to be concerned with. A simple sales tax can pay for this.

We entrust our Government to oversee these areas of our civilization for reasons of efficiency, security and accountability. We place our trust in the Constitution to guide the Government in its managing process.

This process and responsibility of management requires money to function. Money to pay the staff in Government and money to pay for the services they provide us with. To pay for this we consent to paying taxes. A reasonable rate of taxation is reasonable; the money benefits us by providing us with civilization. But when taxes are excessive, prohibitive and downright unjustified – something has to give.

Somewhere along the way Americans went from paying taxes on certain goods to paying State and Local taxes on all goods and services – to paying State and Federal taxes on profits –to paying Income tax – to paying Property tax (which makes the owner of land a tenant to the Government) – to paying Estate taxes - and on and on it goes. The Government is meant to work for you – and more and more it's you working for the Government.

These tax/citizen dollars go to fuel the spending fire of an ever-expanding Government and its programs. Every Board or Department that is created only goes on to cost too much and create miles of unnecessary red tape. If you want a Welfare State, try communism and socialism; just don't be disappointed when you find out they go broke and don't work. Right now the U.S. is a Welfare State and it isn't just going broke – it is broke. What's worse is that people are struggling to get by on what little Government support they do receive.

More taxation isn't going to solve the problem; it's making it worse. We get rid of the excessive taxes we have today by:

- Abolishing income tax.
- Abolishing Payroll taxes, i.e., Social Security (the Government mustn't be concerned with ensuring people save their money for retirement.)
- Abolish far-stretching socially-insured medicine.
- Abolishing Government-insured unemployment benefits in favor of employer-based unemployment insurance.
- Eliminating debt which requires interest payments.
- Eliminating Government programs which cannot be afforded, or that require debt to be afforded.
- Eliminating spending on services that could be purchased out of pocket based on demand; i.e., eliminate services that people should pay and provide for themselves.
- Eliminating the foreign military presence worldwide.
- Eliminating non-emergency foreign aid (this is the work of charities).
- Eliminating subsidies; if a business or industry is not economically viable, it should fold and be replaced by something the market demands or accepts.

We could then help the less fortunate in society, voluntarily and more efficiently, with the tax dollars we save. We have the technology and money to feed, clothe, and shelter the people who can't do this for themselves. And we should. We have the obligation to ensure that people who want, and are able, to work for a prosperous life can have one; not give one to them.

The richer the individual, the richer the country. The richer the Government, the poorer the individual and the poorer the country.

CENTRAL BANKS, WORLD BANK, IMF...

(The following is an excerpt of an e-mail exchange I had with a friend of a friend who used to work for the World Bank.)

As for my thoughts on The Fed, they're pretty simple. I understand that central banks are a benefit to progress. The ability to create money, in turn, creates capital and capital, in turn, provides the oxygen that's essential for productivity and survival in a modern state. There is no doubt about it that fractional reserve banking can "create" more capital than a gold standard and, as such, can create a more productive economy; in the short run of things. But this exchange of abundant capital for sound capital is dangerous. It creates a system of wealth not based on something tangible, but based on... call it paper, zeros, excel sheets, whatever. Whatever it is, it's wealth that can be highly manipulated. It's a kind of wealth that has destroyed many countries in the past and is hurting a lot of people today.

Central banks are predicated on the firm belief that people can regulate them to ward off inflation; that people won't create too much money. Of course people always do create too much*. In the process, currency is devalued and personal and private wealth is lost; the wealthy retain their relative wealth, while the less well-off endure the harsher effects of inflation. In the process, currency is devalued and personal and private wealth is lost. Inflation, whether it's at 1% or 3%, hurts the little guy - big time. And that small amount of inflation is considered a reasonable thing in a central banking system; but when you think of the rate of return the average person gets in a savings account, the harsh reality sets in. For me, at least.

Furthermore, it is believed that central banks are compatible with free markets and that they can even make them sounder. This is ironic because free markets are to be free from external/centralized influences and planning. I believe that people and businesses should be responsible for, and accountable to, their respective borrowing and savings. However, artificially lowering interests rates encourages excessive borrowing and spending that creates dangerous inflation in every facet of the economy. Conversely, artificially increasing interest rates creates excessive strains on borrowers.

* - Here's where I might completely lose you. Central banks are the backbone of a socialist state. At the very least, central banks facilitate reckless governance. A Government cannot spend what it doesn't have. But if it has a printing press, debts and deficit spending are all too easy to rack up. All of the entitlement spending and many wars have been made possible because of the Federal Reserve; there simply isn't enough tax revenue to pay for all of the Government spending going on. $60,000 + debt per working American and people really think central banking, The Fed, and Keynesian economic theory are viable, stable, and realistic? It's a la la land that the Gold Standard wouldn't permit. And that's precisely the reason why it isn't in place. Would China or Japan be willing to ship close to $800 billion, each, in gold bullion over here in containers next to the flatscreens and Dora the Explorer dolls?

As for the World Bank and IMF, my criticisms are just as harsh and I'm sure you've heard them before. I have a problem with foreign aid as it's taking money from Americans and distributing it to other countries in what, by and large, amounts to corporate welfare and/or deposits in Swiss bank accounts. But that's foreign aid. What I don't like about the World Bank and the IMF is the central banking role in it all. Both institutions use money taken from taxpayers, or created by central banks, and lend it out at interest for ostensibly charitable purposes. In theory, it makes sense. Give a poor country money to build infrastructure and social programs. When the funded initiatives pay off, the countries can then pay off their debt. Realistically, these poor countries have great difficulty even servicing the interest on their debt. That, and a lot of aid finds its way to the bank accounts and expense accounts of corrupt leaders. It should also be noted that many of the loans are granted with political and social conditions; conditions that influence countries at the whim of others. As such, loan recipients often end up losing sovereignty.

Have any world aid beneficiaries risen out of poverty and fully paid off their debt? The cruel part of this practice is that money is made off of developing countries while they are still trying to get on their feet. I could understand demanding payment once they established viable economies, but before they even have the running water and high school graduates? I know that banks make money off of these development loans, but do the taxpayers who help fund them? If the interest is simply funnelled back into these institutions I can only see this as making the borrowers slaves. It makes them slaves only because they are working to pay off institutions that didn't do anything to provide them with the money borrowed. The worst part of it all is that the money loaned out, that doesn't come from taxpayers, required no effort to create and has no tangible value. This is the cruel sin of central banking. I could go into how countries that have to renege on payments are forced to sell off resources and assets, but I've made my point.

All of that said, much good has come from the IMF and World Bank. Diseases have been prevented and treated, schools built, infrastructure put in place. I just think a lot of it has come at an exorbitant cost. Poorer countries would be far better off with private investment, donations, volunteer work, and true free trade.

Central banking and foreign aid needs to go and The United States of America must reinstate its own sovereign, tangible currency.

IMMIGRATION

It's what gives people who want to do more with their lives a shot at hope. It's what gives America a vital source of its workforce, ideas and brainpower. Whenever a person complains about the States to me I always ask them why so many people try to immigrate here first. They stumble to find answers like a drunk stumbles to find a keyhole at three in the morning.

Unless you've ever known true poverty, a true lack of educational opportunities, a true lack of access to healthcare, a true lack of personal freedoms, a true lack of any employment opportunities – you can't know why America is the first country of choice for people wanting to immigrate. We all know America isn't perfect. People are homeless, hungry, uneducated, unemployed, medically uninsured, and have a raft of other issues to contend with; like anywhere else in the world.

The way the immigrant sees it is that the homeless person here used to have a home and somewhere in life they lost it by getting sick in the head or through poor financial decisions. The immigrant looks at all of the schools, even the bad ones, and is amazed that they can get access to them, or pay for the ones they want and get scholarships for good grades and effort. An immigrant sees paramedics, ambulances, hospitals, and drugstores as a marvel; and as services they're willing to work for. The immigrant looks at civil rights abuses and attacks on the Constitution (which are terrible) only to remember they couldn't read certain books, travel, or legitimately vote where they came from. The immigrant sympathizes with the unemployed, but realized that at least they had a job, have actual skills, can improve their skills, and can always look for another job. The idea of a place where you can rent a safe apartment or own a home, with clean running water, grocery stores and schools nearby, a place to go to work, a bank to stash some cash in... all of that stuff – it's a pretty wild idea for a lot of people. If an immigrant is lucky, they find a job or start up a business that can provide them with a better life. Most immigrants know, though, that they're really working to give their kids a better go in life.

Talking with immigrant convenience store owners, restaurant owners, hot dog vendors, cab drivers, sanitary workers, construction workers, Eastern Bloc strippers, and all of the immigrants who I've worked shit jobs with over the years woke me up to "immigrant optimism" at a young age.

Immigration only works under two conditions. The first being the desire of the person immigrating to work. This welfare state, socialist mentality of we'll let desperate people come over here and take care of them is nonsense;

all of us as individuals have enough trouble tending to our own affairs, let alone babysitting others through bureaucracies funded with our money. If charity is your cause, donate to agencies that help people overseas before they fly or boat it over. Who or what foreign entity is willing to support American citizens?

The second condition is the flow of immigration. If we didn't have as many welfare services this wouldn't be so much of a problem, but I digress. Wait your turn in line. Granting amnesty to people who have broken the law is an incentive to cut the line; it shouldn't be permitted. If too many people flood the labor market, you get too many people competing for jobs; the result is lower wages and higher unemployment.

Lastly, the taxi driver with a Ph.D., or medical degree nonsense has to end. If someone has valuable skills of any kind, let them prove them and use them to improve their lives. If immigrants with skills can't be permitted to use them, we're depriving the country of useful resources.

INMIGRACIÓN

ES LO QUE DA A LA GENTE QUE QUIERE HACER MAS DE SUS VIDAS UNA OPORTUNIDAD Y ESPERANZA. ES LO QUE DA A ESTADOS UNIDOS UNA FUENTE VITAL DE MANO DE OBRA; IDEAS Y CAPITAL INELECTUAL. CUANDO UNA PERSONA SE QUEJA DE ESTADOS UNIDOS, SIEMPRE LES PREGUNTO EL PORQUE TANTAS PERSONAS BUSCAN IMIGRAR AQUÍ EN PRIMERA. SE TAMBALEAN PARA ENCONTRAR UNA RESPUESTA, IGUAL QUE COMO SE TAMBALEA UN BORRACHO PARA ENCONTRAR UN OJO DE CERRADURA A LAS TRES DE LA MADRUGADA.

A MENOS QUE HAYAS EXPERIMENTADO UNA VERDADERA POBREZA, UNA VERDADERA FALTA DE OPORTUNIDADES ACADÉMICAS, UNA VERDADERA FALTA A ACCESO AL SEGURO SOCIAL, UNA VERADERA FALTA DE GARANTÍAS INDIVIDUALES, UNA VERDADERA FALTA DE OPORTUNIDADES LABORALES- NO SABRÁS POR QUE ESTADOS UNIDOS ES LA PRIMERA OPCIÓN PARA PERSONAS QUE QUIEREN IMIGRAR. TODOS SABEMOS QUE ESTADOS UNIDOS NO ES PERFECTO. HAY VAGABUNDOS EN LA CALLE, CON HAMBRE, SIN EDUCACIÓN, DESEMPLEADOS, SIN SEGURO SOCIAL MÉDICO Y TIENEN MUCHOS OTROS ASUNTOS CON LOS CUALES DEBEN LIDIAR; COMO EN CUALQUIER OTRA PARTE DEL MUNDO.

LA FORMA EN LA QUE EL IMIGRANTE LO VE, ES QUE UN VAGABUNDO AQUÍ, EN ALGÚN MOMENTO TUVO UNA CASA Y EN ALGÚN MOMENTO DE SU VIDA LA PERDIÓ POR ALGUNA ENFERMEDAD MENTAL O POR MALAS DECISIONES FINANCIERAS. EL IMIGRANE VE TODAS LAS ESCUELAS, INCLUSO LAS MALAS, Y SE SORPRENDE DE TENER ACCESO A ELLAS, O PAGAN POR ASISTIR A LAS QUE ELLOS QUIEREN Y CONSIGUEN BECAS POR BUENAS CALIFICACIONES Y ESFUERZO. UN IMIGRANTE VE, PARAMEDICOS, AMBULANCIAS, HOSPITALES, Y FARMACIAS COMO ALGO MARAVILLOSO; Y LOS VEN COMO SERVICIOS POR LOS QUE ESTÁN DISPUESTOS A TRABAJAR PARA TENER ACCESO A ELLOS.

EL IMIGRANTE VE EL ABUSO A LOS DERECHOS CIVILES Y ATAQUES EN LA COSNTITUCIÓN (QUE SON TERRIBLES) SOLO PARA RECORDAR QUE NO PODÍAN LEER CIERTOS LIBROS, VIAJAR, O VOTAR LEGITIMAMENTE EN LOS PAÍSES DE LOS QUE PROVIENEN. EL IMIGRANTE SIMPATIZA CON LOS DESEMPLEADOS, SIN EMBARGO, SE DA CUENTA QUE AL MENOS TENÍAN UN TRABAJO, TIENEN HABILIDADES, PUEDEN MEJORAR ESAS HABILIDADES, Y SIEMPRE PUEDEN BUSCAR UN NUEVO TRABAJO. LA IDEA DE UN LUGAR EN EL QUE PUEDES RENTAR UN DEPARTAMENTO SEGURO O SER DUEÑO DE SU PROPIA CASA, CON AGUA DE LA LLAVE LIMPIA, TIENDAS DE ABARROTES Y ESCUELAS CERCANAS, UN LUGAR DONDE TRABAJAR, UN BANCO PARA DEPOSITAR ALGO DE DINERO… TODAS ESAS COSAS- SON UNA GRAN IDEA PARA MUCHAS PERSONAS. SI UN IMIGRANTE TIENE SUERTE, PUEDEN ENCONTRAR UN TRABAJO O INICIAR SU PROPIO NEGOCIO, QUE LES PERMITIRÁ TENER UNA MEJOR VIDA. SIN EMBARGO, LA MAYORÍA DE LOS IMIGRANTES SABEN QUE ESTÁN TRABAJANDO PARA OFRECER MEJORES OPORTUNIDADES DE VIDA A SUS HIJOS.

HABLANDO CON IMIGRANTES DUEÑOS DE TIENDAS DE CONVENIENCIA, DUEÑOS DE RESTAURANTES, VENDEDORES EN PUESTOS DE HOT DOGS, TAXISTAS, TRABAJADORES DE INTENDENCIA, ALBAÑILES, DESNUDISTAS DE EUROPA ORIENTAL, Y TODOS LOS IMIGRANTES CON LOS QUE A LO LARGO DE LOS AÑOS HE COMPARTIDO TRABAJOS DE MIERDA, ME DEJARON VER A UNA EDAD TEMPRANA, EL "OPTIMISMO IMIGRANTE".

LA IMIGRACIÓN SOLO TRABAJA BAJO DOS CONDICIONES. LA PRIMERA ES EL DESEO DE LA PERSONA DE IMIGRAR PARA TRABAJAR. ESTA MENTALIDAD SOCIALISTA, DE ESTADO DE BIENESTAR, DE DEJAR QUE LA GENTE VENGA Y NOSOTROS NOS ENCARGAMOS DE ELLOS NO TIENE SENTIDO; TODOS NOSOTROS COMO INDIVIDUOS TENEMOS SUFICIENTES PROBLEMAS OCUPÁNDONOS DE NUESTROS PROPIOS ASUNTOS, DEJEMOS A UN LADO CUIDAR DE LOS DEMÁS A TRAVÉS DE LA BUROCRACIA SOPORTADA CON NUESTRO DINERO. SI TU FUNCIÓN ES LA CARIDAD, HAZ DONACIONES A AGENCIAS QUE AYUDEN A LAS PERSONAS EN SUS PAÍSES DE ORIGEN ANTES DE QUE VUELEN O SE EMBARQUEN PARA LLEGAR HASTA ACA. QUIÉN O QUE ENTIDAD EXTRANJERA ESTÁ DISPUESTA A APOYAR A CIUDADANOS ESTADOUNIDENSES?

LA SEGUNDA CONDICIÓN ES EL FLUJO DE IMIGRANTES. SI NO TUVIÉRAMOS TANTOS SERVICIOS DE BIENESTAR ESTO NO SERÍA UN PROBLEMA TAN COMPLEJO, PERO YO DIFIERO. ESPERA TU TURNO EN LA FILA. OTORGAR AMNESTÍA A LA GENTE QUE HA VIOLADO LA LEY ES UN INCENTIVO PARA BRINCARSE LA FILA; NO DEBERÍA PERMITIRSE. SI MUCHAS PERSONAS INUNDAN EL MERCADO LABORAL, TE ENCUENTRAS CON MUCHAS PERSONAS COMPITIENDO POR TRABAJOS; EL RESULTADO ES SUELDOS MAS BAJOS Y MAS DESEMPLEO.

FINALMENTE, EL SIN SENTIDO DEL TAXISTA CON DOCTORADO O TÍTULO DE MÉDICO TIENE QUE TERMINAR. SI ALGUIÉN TIENE HABILIDADES VALIOSAS DE CUALQUIER ÍNDOLE, DÉJALOS PROVARLAS Y USARLAS PARA MEJORAR SU NIVEL DE VIDA. SI A LOS IMIGRANTES CON HABILIDADES NO SE LES PERMITE USARLAS, ESTAMOS LIMITANDO AL PAÍS DE RECURSOS Y HABILIDADES ÚTILES.

TERRORISM

Terrorism is violence carried out by people who do not wear uniforms and, or, don't fight under a flag. Terrorism almost always has a political objective, usually accompanied with a religious grievance that aims to change policy or ease oppression. For the sake of time we'll cut to the chase and deal with the kind of Terrorism that most Americans are concerned with – Militant Islam.

There are a few Muslims who see Islam as under attack because of Western cultural, economic, political, and militaristic influences in "lands" that are Muslim; lands that should be free of these influences. These same people see Israel as an American front, if you will. They use their interpretation of a book to convince people of all levels of education that America and its allies are a devil to be crushed by the true believers of God. The fact that at any given time you can turn on the Arab news channel Aljazeera and see American soldiers firing bullets at, and dropping bombs on, Muslims only helps these militant mindsets; helps them in their conviction and recruitment. The fact that there are U.S. military bases in Muslim "lands" pisses the general population off in general.

The result is that you get some people eager to lash out. They can't form an army, so they resort to the next best thing they can; terrorism, i.e., small-scale attacks with the effect of full scale armed conflict. The problem with Militant Islam is that it doesn't have a set objective just to get foreigners off of and out of Muslim lands; it states that Judgment Day cannot come until everyone on earth is a Muslim. I know, it's a big problem... millions of Westerners don't have the desire to take up a new faith.

These kooks believe that the law of their holy book should be followed by everyone. And these assholes want all of the protections that Western civilization affords religion, to try and dissolve our separation of church and state; the very thing that protects religious freedoms, among others. These people don't understand that in America (or any other civilized nation) you can't kill your daughter because she likes cosmetics, prefers wearing a baseball hat on her head in public, listens to Hillary Duff and Miley Cyrus (granted that could be considered in poor taste) and wants to hang out with friends from different upbringings; no matter how much it offends your honor.

There's not much that can be done about this, apart from having an educated populous and keeping these nut jobs on the other side of either ocean. Trying to democratize the Muslim "lands" or fight off the nut jobs with our

Armed Forces will only cause death, financial ruin, and more of the same problem – resentment. At home, we preserve our laws and system of Government. And we don't let people from foreign lands with regressive cultures tell us how we should live and what we must do.

I'm one of these weird people who didn't see September 11, 2001 as an act or declaration of war. The event was equivalent to things that happen during wars. But it wasn't carried out by a country or an army; the only two things that can declare a formal war. Instead of negotiating with a rogue cult-like Government and taking about a month to invade Afghanistan, I truly believe we'd have all been safer sending in about 100 hardcore motherfucking Rambos. They should have been flown in the same night of the attacks, subdued any Taliban, and separated the culprits from the followers. But that would have been too easy, intelligent and unprofitable. And it would have been lacking the revenge and fireworks a lot of people wanted. In reality, the FBI, CIA, NSA, and other agencies that may exist, having the best brains and technology at their disposal, are the safest solutions for both the prevention and response to terrorism.

I say that because it is inevitable that a bomb or attack of some kind will happen again in America. When it does, people have to understand you don't retaliate against insanity with more of the same. Armies can't respond to a subway bomb. It's not a response, it's a mess. You keep morale high, by picking up the pieces, living life and bringing the criminals to justice – that's it.

I am a firm believer that once the United States Armed Forces are withdrawn from the Middle East, and Governments within the Middle East are either no longer supported by the United States or no longer have oil to sell, the youth will revolt, and Militant Islam will eventually fall in on itself; it will have to fight rational Muslims.

CHINA

風
林
火
山

I hate spreading fear with the what if's and could be's, but there is a something I shouldn't leave out here. A fair bit of this book has been dedicated to issues and ideas that are directly relevant to Americans. But we shouldn't get caught too far off with our heads too far up our asses.

The gravest threat to everyone in the world isn't disease, oil reserves, money, water, or a handful of lost religious nut jobs. I'm calling it now and I hope it gets out. The biggest threat in the world is the Chinese Government. Not the people of the country, but the people who control it. Not the people who serve in its army, but the people who tell them what to do.

The Asian culture is one which deprives the individual of ego and, as a consequence, deprives the individual of a sense of freedom, yet effectively instils the individual with a sense of purpose. Pride and honor are prized and coveted ideals to our friends in the Orient. You know that military mindset, the very serious dudes with their codes and obligations to live up to them? That's what I mean. It's a pretty serious culture. Case in point is how the Chinese despise the Japanese for two simple things (though many will not openly admit to it) – getting beat up in wars and invasions, and Japan's rise to manufacturing excellence. A better example is how diligent most Asian kids are. They're taught that North American kids are lazy, spoiled, disrespectful and undisciplined. A lot of pressure is placed on Asian kids to outperform Westerners. I'm sure we've all had an Asian buddy or classmate who's recalled the classic story of getting physically beaten by his father for a bad grade of 88%; I've heard of two that involved golf clubs.

The Chinese culture doesn't just want to be good and prosperous - it wants to be on top of the world. And its sense of pride and saving face will not permit anything short of this. But, we need to remember that it is the Chinese Government that sets the goals; the people follow because they are taught to.

The hounds are unleashed and gaining ground. China is well on its way to becoming the biggest economy and military force in the world.

Where we need to be worried is if China runs out of resources to fuel and maintain its worldly girth, and when and where its first display of military ascendency, might be. The new guy is going to show everyone how big his gun is some day. We think we know how much the Chinese Government has in its arms cache, but do you really think it divulges the actual figures and sums of money it spends on armaments? If the CIA knew, it wouldn't tell us anyway.

Why the U.S. doesn't trade with Cuba, but does with the largest communist dictatorship and official violator of human rights in the world isn't a mystery; it's proof in print of Government hypocrisy and its interference in private enterprise. In the last twenty-five years we sold out our economy for inferior consumer goods.

Propping up a corrupt land of oppression, like doing it without a rubber because it feels good in the moment, will leave us sore in the end. It's just a matter of time until we all realize it.

It is my sincere hope and firm belief that a demonstrated overhauling of the American political system, carried out by the people who it represents, can and will set an example to the people of the world, both free and dictated to, so that they can improve their homes, communities and societies; not with the sacrifice of life and pain, but with the conscious and seldom-employed forces of logic and reason.

REVOLUTION

The Genius of the Crowd

there is enough treachery, hatred violence absurdity in the average
human being to supply any given army on any given day

and the best at murder are those who preach against it
and the best at hate are those who preach love
and the best at war finally are those who preach peace

those who preach god, need god
those who preach peace do not have peace
those who preach peace do not have love

beware the preachers
beware the knowers
*beware those who are always reading books**
beware those who either detest poverty
or are proud of it
beware those quick to praise
for they need praise in return
beware those who are quick to censor
they are afraid of what they do not know
beware those who seek constant crowds for
they are nothing alone
beware the average man the average woman
beware their love, their love is average
seeks average

but there is genius in their hatred
there is enough genius in their hatred to kill you
to kill anybody
not wanting solitude
not understanding solitude
they will attempt to destroy anything
that differs from their own
not being able to create art
they will not understand art
they will consider their failure as creators
only as a failure of the world
not being able to love fully
they will believe your love incomplete
and then they will hate you
and their hatred will be perfect

like a shining diamond
like a knife
like a mountain
like a tiger
like hemlock
their finest art

**Professors*

Charles Bukowski (1920-1994)

The United States of America was founded not as a nation that would meet people's needs, but as a nation that would enable people to meet their needs as independent and free people. The United States of America was founded to provide people with the right to life, liberty, and the pursuit of happiness. The Constitution of The United States of America was created and adopted as the supreme law of the nation, to defend people's life, liberty, pursuit of happiness, and The United States of America. The following is an account of the many offences to the lives, liberties, and pursuits of Americans, and the Constitution of The United States of America:

Our Government is committed to building and maintaining military bases around the world at the expense of its citizens' wealth and security, without their consent.

Our Government has waged an illegal war and has repeatedly misinformed its citizens' of the conflict's cause, cost, and plan for its conclusion.

Our Government has spied on its citizens.

Our Government has engaged in the practice of torture, distorting words and laws to ensure impunity for those who authorize and employ such a practice.

Our Government is arresting and detaining people without charges or proper legal counsel and due process.

Our Government has arrested and seized the assets and wealth of citizens acting in accordance with the laws of their State.

Our Government is burdening its citizens with debt accumulated from profligate spending, and the subsequent taxation and borrowing to pay for it.

Our Government is compromising the sovereignty of The United States of America by spending its way into the debt of foreign nations.

Our Government is committed to economic and military treaties that threaten and limit the sovereignty of its citizens by obligating them to trade and act in terms that may, or may not be, dictated to them.

Our Government is carrying out warrantless and undue search and seizures of property.

Our Justice System is impotent in prosecuting the politically connected. It is also ineffective in prosecuting and upholding laws against businesses with deep pockets.

Our Justice System recognizes and grants incorporations the same rights and freedoms of sentient human beings.

Our Government prohibits the free sale and exchange of substances which it cannot control, or deems unfit for consumption.

Our Government imprisons and fines its citizens for consuming or possessing substances which it does not control, or deems unfit for consumption.

Our Government's pursuit of economic growth and favorable foreign relations entails the tyrannical tactics of manipulating other nations' political processes, aiding despots, issuing economic threats, the implementing of economic embargoes, and issuing threats of military intervention.

Our elected officials ensure benefits for themselves that they do not ensure for the citizens who elected them; benefits that should be paid for by our elected officials themselves, if they wish, and not by the State, i.e., citizens.

Our Government has stifled its citizens' ability to protest grievances; cordoning off public property at major political events, in favor of the ridiculous concept of "free speech zones." There should be no public property precluded to, or public property specifically limited to, free speech in a free nation.

Our Government is increasingly militarizing our municipal police forces for its own interest.

Our Government is beholden to international economic and military treaties that limit the sovereignty of The United States of America.

Our Government has proven that it is unable to provide adequate response and relief to national emergencies and disasters.

Our Government is engaged in illegal bribery through the practice of lobbying.

The Electoral College is past its time of purpose. An anachronistic system, it does not represent or serve justice to the will of the individual citizen who votes.

Our election process is unsound. Machines, of any kind, must not be allowed to participate in any Government election process.

Our elected officials, more increasingly, win office not based on their ideas and integrity, but based on their ability to raise and spend money. The seeds of fascism are planted, when corporations can finance individuals into elected positions.

Our Government does not protect the wealth of its citizens' natural resources adequately. For those businesses that destroy any of these resources, the fines, on account of their relative leniency, merely amount to additional taxes or tax write-off opportunities.

Our Government allows a two party system to dominate control and influence over the three branches of Government. This is permitted by both parties, and only both parties, determining who can, and cannot, debate according to unreasonable standards.

The Executive Branch is circumventing the checks and balances of the Legislative and Judicial Branches with the use of Executive Privilege.

The Executive Branch is using Signing Statements and Executive Orders to circumvent the checks and balances of the Legislative and Judicial Branches.

Our Government has allowed our currency to be wekened by replacing sound commodity-backed money with a paper money system that creates inflation and a loss of wealth as citizen wages, salaries and expenditure of time and energy do not increase at an even pace with the cost of goods and services.

The ability of Government and banks to create money out of nothing with this system affords irresponsible Government spending on entitlement programs, wars and reckless lending practices.

Our Government has granted the authority of our currency and free market interest rates, not to its citizens, but to a power that is not accountable to the American people or the elected officials who represent them.

Our Government infringes on the freedom of its citizens by forcibly collecting and redistributing their earned money, without individual consent, under the slogan of "for the good of the people." This is a principle of communism and socialism; both of which infringe on life, liberty and the pursuit of happiness.

Our Government is increasingly interfering with its citizens' businesses by imposing regulations that infringe on the principles of free markets.

Our Government is spending its citizens' money to assist failed businesses and the individuals who failed them.

Our Government now owns parts of, and advises the management of, large businesses; a dangerous course of conduct and a precedent that will ensure more of the same in the future.

Our Government is engaged in economic planning and lawmaking that is influenced by, and desirable to, certain businesses. This is fascism. A free market cannot exist within such conditions.

Our Government employs a paramilitary organization that is unaccountable to our elected representatives.

Our President has been granted the authority to declare citizens as Enemy Combatants, and to have their Rights revoked. A dangerous concept and charge, that is applicable to foreign and domestic citizens, it can be wielded by the President, exempt from the purview of the Judicial and Legislative Branches.

Our ability to rectify these grievances through the electoral process has been proven ineffectual. Revolution, as a means to rectify these grievances, is necessary and justified. The following is an excerpt from the Declaration of Independence which offers validation for such a cause:

We hold these truths to be self-evident, that **all men are** created **equal**, that they are endowed by their Creator **with certain** unalienable **Rights**, **that** among these **are Life**, **Liberty and the pursuit of Happiness**. That **to secure these rights**, **Governments are instituted** among Men, deriving their just powers from the consent of the governed, That **whenever any Form of Government becomes destructive of these ends**, it is the Right of **the People** to (**alter or** to **abolish it**), and to institute new Government, laying its foundation on such principles and organizing its powers in such form, as to them shall seem most likely **to effect their Safety and Happiness**.

Pay particular attention to the words out of the *Declaration of Independence* that are in emphasis. Does our Government need to be altered or abolished? If we were living under a truly oppressive regime, then yes, there would be a case made to abolish our Government; throw every bum out of office by any and every means, and then start from scratch. But we're living in a country that is only leading us towards a road of total oppression; by oppression I mean a Government that becomes completely deaf to the voice of the citizenry, and works to meet the desires of the highest bidders and its own interests exclusively. We're not there yet, but we're well on our way, as the grievances herein attest to.

Certainly there are Government practices and policies that need to be altered and abolished. To return to a principled and sound Nation our Government must:

Abolish the Patriot Act and any legislation that infringes on the Constitution and Bill of Rights.

End the reckless concept of pre-emptive war.

End the practice of torture in any and all its forms.

End economic sanctions against countries; a practice that cripples people under such limitations, and encourages support for tyrants and hatred towards The United States of America and its citizens.

End support for the United Nations, The World Bank, and the International Monetary Fund by ceasing to fund them with any and all taxpayer money.

Abolish the taxation of incomes; people are not workers for the state.

Rely on sales taxes to finance its institutions and projects.

End non-emergency foreign aid to Governments (this is the business of private citizens and charities).

End the amnesty afforded to illegal immigrants. For decades immigrants have risked death to get to The United States of America and build a better life. Now many people risk death for welfare entitlements.

Abolish the Federal Reserve System. It is the epitome of the kind of banking that has sacked every other great nation in history. Phase it out in favor of money backed by gold and/or silver.

Abolish Central Banking principles and practices.

End spending on things that can't be afforded.

Phase out Social Security, Medicare, Medicaid, and other services that are bankrupting the nation.

Let citizens decide how to save their money, access and purchase their healthcare, and how to support services for the less fortunate.

End wars that are illegal and that cannot be afforded.

End all military allegiances with foreign Governments.

End the practice of selling off debt and borrowing from foreign Governments.

Respect the authority of Sates and their laws.

Legalize drugs.

End the practice of lobbying.

Only consider or vote on legislation that has been drafted by elected officials.

Remove the control of elections from any and all Political Parties.

Limit campaign financing to private, non-corporate, donations.

Lower the minimum polling standards candidates must meet to qualify for political debates.

End the Electoral College and decide elections based on the popular vote.

Preclude machines from the election process. People vote and people should be left to count those votes.

Subject Executive Privilege to the scrutiny and approval of the Judicial Branch.

End the practice of Executive Orders and Signing Statements and repeal any existing orders and statements that have not been subject to the scrutiny and approval of the Legislative and Judicial Branches.

Repeal corporate personhood.

Cease subsidizing industry of any kind, in any manner.

Prosecute individuals who knowingly permit or withhold information regarding illegal corporate conduct, in addition to fining the corporation they represent and/or work for.

Prosecute all people equally, to the fullest extent of the law, regardless of political clout or social standing.

End the support of dictators and other scourges to humanity, for the sake of geopolitical and economic influence.

Police the borders of The United States of America with force. Not the world.

Prohibit any paramilitary activity or organizations.

Revoke the entitlement benefits of elected officials.

Safeguard appointed positions by strictly yielding and adhering to ethics; rejecting all persons with conflicts of interest, both past and present.

Sounds impossible, right? How can this be accomplished? You do it by starting a revolution. For years people have taken Government abuse and Government-backed corporate abuse. For years they take it, accept it, and then forget about it. The abuse ends when you demonstrate that you're not going to sit back and let it continue to happen. It ends when people stop listening to the assurances of men who read speeches they didn't write; and, instead, start listening to their hearts and reason. It ends by voting out inactive career politicians and voting in qualified people of integrity. The abuse ends by taking responsibility for your own actions. It ends by learning and talking about it. It ends by thinking for yourself. And then you act.

How does this revolution play out? With guns and blood? Nope. By joining a party of any kind? Any formal group or association, which both have the burden of requiring money and volunteering to sustain them, can be marginalized in any number of ways, thereby preventing or delegitimizing any action. So not that either.

A revolution requires three things to succeed. 1. The will of the people. 2. A course of action that has a strong chance of achieving a set objective. 3. The will of the people to support and stay the course of action.

If people want their Government to reform its ways, they have to pressure it. By pressuring it, the many good people representing you in Government will be empowered to speak up and act out against the many corrupt and misguided politicians in Government. An environment of pressure will expose the Government for what it is, warts and all. This exposure leads to disclosure. Disclosure leads to real reform. Not an overnight fix-all, but the environment for gradual reform... an awakening.

How do you pressure a Government? When millions of people march on Washington... the Government will feel pressure. Do these people march in protest, chanting slogans, and hope that someone will listen to them? Nope. They walk up to the buildings, to the White House, to Capitol Hill, to the Pentagon. They walk up in a slow and peaceful manner and stick their grievances and resolutions to the walls or fences of these buildings. Or they leave them on the ground around these buildings. And then they go home.

The media reports it live and the world watches. And then the politicians have a problem. Do they appease the people by acting on their demands, or do they give them more lip service? The second option could very well lead to an all-out revolt. Failure to act thoroughly could also lead to civil unrest. When a Government is pressured, good people within it can have their day. Laws, attitudes and direction will be forced to alter their course.

If millions of people descend on the capital of the most powerful nation in the world in peaceful protest, and the rest of the world sees this take place... the possibilities are endless. Citizens of weaker and corrupt nations might take cue and overthrow dictatorships and oppressive regimes. Citizens of other countries might actually clue in and realize that if they can mobilize, they don't have to be pushed around any longer. They might see there is hope to take control of their destiny. You can't predict these things with certainty, but a peaceful revolution here could send shock waves around the globe.

Make no mistake, the Government is, and the interests that influence are, extremely afraid of this possible scenario. Government has only three options it can hope for to preserve its current state and avoid having a revolution on its hands.

1. Discredit the notion of a massive gathering as foolish, a threat to Homeland Security, a threat to the economy, and potentially dangerous for the people in the crowds. This is the use of fear, a tactic Government employs relentlessly against people to gain support and quash dissent. We've seen it used ad nauseam over the last decade. It's bullshit.

2. They can crack down on the march like they do at conventions, by simply blockading areas of interest to the people. But the Government lacks the manpower and resources to block off the better part of a city from tens of millions of moving people. Trying to stop people from advancing with the use of force would look bad for a number of reasons. Firstly, it would be illegal and anti-democratic. Secondly, does the Government want to look like the regime in Iran? Do they want this while the world is watching? The Government simply has to sit back while democracy is exercised. All while the world is watching.

Should the Government try and prevent a march, only the Government has to worry. If we live in a free country, surely you should be able to walk through the streets of its capital? If riot police and military forces are set up to deny you the right to protest in your own country, don't get mad or angry with them; they're only doing they're job. Just leave your grievances and resolutions on the ground in front of them. With any luck, the men and women who may be forced to obstruct the march might just stand down.

But again, a Government simply can't get in the way of tens of millions of peaceful people.

3. There will be people in Government, and citizens as well, who will hope for this to fold in on itself. I'm a realist. Tens of millions of people walking through a city could have some serious consequences. But being aware of these consequences is the best way to avert them. If people are given a 24-hour window to walk up to a building and leave a couple of pieces of paper behind, things should run smoothly. People should come and go – there is nothing more dangerous than an idle crowd; before you know it, an idiot tosses a rock and then everyone gets in trouble. Be cool, be calm, and think for yourself. As to how this can be organized, it can't. If people show up to Washington and walk through the streets in a peaceful manner, I'm sure everyone would be able to post their grievances and resolutions on at least one building of their choosing; if you can't even reach one building, don't worry about it. At least you showed up.

Anarchists will inevitably show up and try to do the dumb shit they do; hurl things and damage property. It's for douchebags like these people that some form of police presence is needed and welcomed. Anarchists are Social outcasts. They hate the system and have no solutions. They hate the system because they are losers in it and fail to realize that even in "the system" they are free to do as they please. The catch is you have to work in life for what you please; and work is something these people aren't fond of. Apart from the delusional dream world of harmonious chaos – the only philosophy these people can identify with is communism. This isn't a day for people who hate Government or what it stands for – it's a day for people who hate the way a democratically elected Government is allowing itself to function. If you see people trying to destroy anything or covering their face to avoid being identified, please surround them and bring them to the police. These morons always get away with their antics because good people simply stand by and watch. If able-bodied people don't prevent these people from causing destruction – the Government will have an excuse to try and disrupt the day's event.

While I'm all for the Second Amendment, don't bring any weapons; this is intended to be peaceful. If tensions were to ever arise they might come into the equation. Guns on show or concealed, when there isn't the presence of an immediate threat, make most people uneasy. And I also suspect that people with guns at a congregation of this size and with its intent, could probably be detained for all kinds of infractions. Remember, the world is watching, don't fuck it up. Fuck it up, and the forces against free people are validated and win. And also remember that your Government is not the enemy. The way it is being run is an adversarial affront to the people it is meant to serve.

The only sacrifice you'll have to make to participate in this is your travel time and expenses. As for when this day should occur, a work-free Government holiday and day with extreme symbolism like July 4th would be more than fitting. What year a revolution will take place is up to you.

Visit: www.the-unitedstates-of-america.com to vote.

A Republic founded on freedom has been weakened by its Government to the extent that a communist dictatorship is well on the way to becoming the wealthiest and best armed nation in the world (in 15 years time or sooner). That's a tragic reality.

Unlike what happened with Russia, we will not be able to successfully fight warm (real, but not fully declared) wars with or "spend" China out of a Cold War. The American dollar isn't going to have the influence it has always had much longer, if it's even in existence in the future. Civil liberties are only going to be further infringed upon. Taxes never go down, they know only one direction. More war is the way of the future. Prices are only rising, people are getting poorer, and there's no money to provide for them as some would like.

If you're tired of talk, here's your chance to act. In the event that people's perceptions can't be changed and a revolution doesn't happen, then it wasn't meant to be. If that's the case, neither was this nation.

Let the country know when you want to get started:

www.the-unitedstates-of-america.com

BIBLIOGRAPHY

Aaboe, Asger. "On Babylonian Planetary Theories." *Centaurus* 5 (1958): 209-77.

Ackrill,J.L *Aristotle the Philosopher.* Oxford: Clarendon Press, 1981.

Adams, Marilyn McCord. *William Ockham*, 2 vols. Notre Dame, Ind.: University of Notre Dame Press, 1987.

Archimedes. *Archimedes in the Middle Ages*, ed. and trans. Marshall Clagett, 5 vols. Madison: University of Wisconsin Press, 1964; Philadelphia: American Philosophical Society, 1976-1984. ------ *The Works of Archimedes: Edited in Modern Notation, with Introductory Chapters*, ed. Thomas L. Heath, 2d ed. Cambridge: Cambridge University Press, 1912.

Ashworth, William B. Jr. "Natural History and the Emblematic World View." In Lindberg, David C., and Westman, Robert S., eds, *Reappraisals of the Scientific Revolution*, pp. 303-32. Cambridge: Cambridge University Press, 1990.

Basalla, George, ed. *The Rise of Modern Science: Internal or External Factors?* Lexington, Mass.: D.C. Health, 1968.

Benson, Robert L., and Constable, Giles, eds. *Renaissance and Renewal in the Twelfth Century.* Cambridge, Mass.: Harvard University Press, 1982.

Benton, John. "Trotula, Women's Problems, and the Professionalization of Medicine in the Middle Ages." *Bulletin of the History of Medicine* 59 (1985): 30-53.

Brain, Peter. Galen on *Bloodletting: A Study of the Origins*, Development and Validity of His Opinions, with a Translation of the Three Works. Cambridge: Cambridge University Press, 1986.

Bynum, Carolyn Walker. *"Did the Twelfth Century Discover the Individual?"* Journal of Ecclesiastical History 31 (1980): 1-17.

Courtenay, William J. Capacity and Volition: *A History of the Distinction of Absolute and Ordained Power.* Quodlibet: Ricerche e strumenti di filosofia medieval, no. 8. Bergamo: Pierluigi Lubrina, 1990.

D'Alverny, Marie-Therese. *"Translations and Translators."* In Benson, Robert L., and Constable, Giles, eds., *Renaissance and Renewal* in the Twelfth Century, pp. 421-62. Cambridge, Mass.: Harvard University Press, 1982.

Drake, Stillman. "*The Uniform Motion Equivalent of a Uniformly Accelerated Motion from Rest.*" Isis 63 (1972): 28-38.

Good, Jack. *The Domestication of the Savage Mind.* Cambridge: Cambridge University Press, 1977.

Grant, Edward. "Medieval and Seventeenth-Century *Conceptions of an Infinite Void Space beyond the Cosmos.*" Isis 60 (1969): 39-60.

Knowles, David. *The Evolution of Medieval Thought.* New York: Vintage, 1964.

Kuhn, Thomas S. *The Copernican Revolution: Planetary Astronomy in the Development of Western Thought.* Cambridge: Harvard University Press, 1957.

Majno, Guido. *The Healing Hand: Man and Wound in the Ancient World.* Cambridge, Mass.: Harvard University Press, 1975.

Morris, Collin. *The Discovery of the Individual,* 1050-1200. New York: Harper and Row, 1972.

Multhauf, Robert P. *The Origins of Chemistry.* New York: Franklin Watts, 1967.

Plutarch: Moralia, Volume V, Isis and Osiris. The E at Delphi. The Oracles at Delphi No Longer Given in Verse. *The Obsolescence of Oracles.* (Loeb Classical Library No. 306): Osiris 1 (1936).

Reynolds, Terry S. Stronger Than a Hundred Men: *A History of the Vertical Water Wheel.* Baltimore: Johns Hopkins University Press, 1983.

Vickers, Brian, ed. *Occult and Scientific Mentalities in the Renaissance.* Cambridge: Cambridge University Press, 1984.

Manic, Depressives. *And Schizophrenics Have a Markedly Enhanced.* Ability to derive,1978. Associations between words, *Places, Events, Objects,* (1923): 12-18.

People, Emotions. And Behaviour.: Volume 6, The thought processes which facilitate: These Associations Break Ground. (For creative exploration: New York: in any number of disciplines), 1902.

Both, Subjective. *And Objective. The Ideas Generated From A Manic,* Depressive, ISSUE: 69 - Or Schizophrenic Episode ------ *Can Be Analysed And Determined* to be Sound or. Chicago: Penguin, 1975.

Delusional, The. *Sound Ideas can be used to Positive Affect* in a Reality. 500 B.C.-300B.C. Where They *Were Once Unrealized*: New York: Dolphin, 1999.

Psychedelic, Drugs. *Can Provide Standard Minds with Access,* Vol X. (347).: If Not Even Greater Access, 1968, *To the Psychotic* and *Altered Perceptions* Experienced by Manic Depressives and. New York: Yankees, 1978.

Schizophrenics, While. *Much of the Ideas Experienced During a Drug* Induced State. Are Useless (upon return to reality), pp. 456-1003: Some *Can Prove.* To be Valid and Life Enhancing. New York: Simon Says, 1995.

For, Centuries. *Manic Depressives and Schizophrenics Have Been* Confined. Cambridge: Cambridge University Press, 1902. Against Their Will, (sec 5, par 18) Subjected to Cruel Treatments. Feared, Loathed and *Misunderstood.* New York: Harpo Harper, 1984.

For, Decades. *Psychedelic Drugs Have Been Illegal,* Feared, Loathed and Misunderstood. For Millennia, (1988): All Three Have. New York: Rangers, 1992.

Been, Making. *Contributions to the Evolution of the Human Species.* Pp. 78-89. While It's Nice To – (sec. 708). New York: Dolphin, 1976.

Romanticise, Manic. *Depression and Schizophrenia Can Ruin the Lives* of Those With. 3 vols. Such afflictions, (1982).: *As Well as* Their Families. New York: Penguin Classics, 1982.

And, Friends. *These Conditions Lead People into Joblessness,* Drug Abuse, Homelessness, Suicide... ISBN: 98736-9874. You name it. (1994).: Vol XII.

Using, Psychedelic. *Drugs Can Land You in Jail and Can Manifest Underlying*, Previously Non-Existent, Seattle, Washington: 1876. Mental Conditions. Order No. 987463HGD376.

The, Best. *Few Minutes of Solitude I Have Ever Had* in my Life Were Some Time. In the Early Fall of 2003. New York: Bruce Wayne, 1971.

Sitting, On. *A Park Bench. The Temperature* Was So Perfect You Didn't Have to Comment. (1956). *On it and the sun was setting*. New York: Simon Does, 1998.

It, Was. *Then and There that it Occurred to me that we and Everything Are*. a part of god. Vol 1. (1999). It Was Also Then – ibid - *That it Wasn't* Occurring To Me That I Was Waging a Fight. New York: Harper Collins, 1999.

Against, The. *Pressures of Reality that I'd Eventually Lose*. After Fixating. Issue 22. On This *Seemingly Profound* Revelation For a While, all I: Philadelphia: Long Press, 1946.

Could, Do. *Was Smile and Feel the Strong Rushes of Energy Flowing Throughout my Body*. ISBN: 9729HG98736. (1972). I stared: New York: Simon Did, 1987.

And, Smiled. *At the Sun so Intensely that Everything Around me Developed Auras*. ed.: And Then (12-18), True to Fucked up Form, New York: I Began to Cry, 1923.

Knowing, Feeling. *This, What Was For me a New Truth*, With Such Intensity Made it so Hard to Look. Roger & Ebert. Vol 6 - *At The People Walking by*; Huntington Printers, 1956.

Realizing, That. *A World Where Such a Thing is Not Understood and Felt is a World Squandered*, Ignorant, And One Not Worth Existing. New York: Metropolitan, 1989.

In, Hindsight. *I Know That the Idea This Book Opened Up With*. Isn't All That New; ISSUE: 9872hgs – (1782). *Some Hindu Mystic, Or A Group Of Them*, Stumbled Upon It Eons Ago. Kashmir: Wilderness, 3,000B.C.E.

But, I. *Know the Way I've Proven it is New and it's Accurate*. Pp. 28-467. Unknown Publisher.

If, Anything. *Sticks in People's Minds After Reading This, I Hope it's the God Shit.* Pp. 87-98. A Couple Of Months Later. New York: Dodgers, 1933.

Running, On. *About Two to Three Hours of Sleep a Day, I Walked Down* to a Friend's Place In.(1898-1912). New York: Askworks, 1912.

Tribecca, While. *It Was Three or Four in the Morning, my Unannounced Visits Were Common.* Vol. 3-5. And At This point I Had No. New York: Penguin Flight, 1684.

Insight, Into. *What Others Would Rightfully Consider Weird and Imposing.* No.: 987. When I Made It Up To Her Place And Sat Down I – New York: Simon Dictates, 1939.

Was, Mumbling. *I Had Been Thinking All Day About How Beautiful the World Was.* I Told Sec. 76 Part:98. Her something *about blowjobs* and that I Thought I Was Pretty Sure I. New York: Simon & Obedience, 1981.

Was, Autistic. *(Really, I Had Just Unassumingly Broken the Ego Barrier; I Knew Who I Was and What Things Were, But I Felt No Personal Connection to Them).* (1205-1206). New York: Penguin Huddle on 4, 1978.

She, Started. *Crying, Offered me a Place to Sleep, Then Went to Bed on the Assumption That I Was Just Fucked on something.* (1789) On Drugs. Vol. 8 - And Then the Worst Thing That Could Happen, New York: Pro-Life, Child Abusers, 1945.

Happened, Naturally. *I Listened to a Song That I Interpreted to be a "Sign" That I Was Right About All the Things I Had. Been Thinking About* (909 A.D.) Ever since my time in the park. New York: Thinking Brain Dog, 1989.

I, Left. *Her Place and Ventured Out Into the Streets, in a Blended State of Bliss and Exhaustion.* Pp. 36-42. I Felt Vindicated – ISBS: 109828GJ233, And Was Certain That by Following the Green Stoplights I Would Discover a Parked Limo, With my Father Inside, Ready to Take me Home. I must - New York: Harp and Xylophone, 1973.

Have, Mistaken. *A Red Light For a Green Somewhere.* I Never Found the Limo. Vol. 77-88: Instead I Ended Up at What (17-23-17-24). *Was Once the Foundation of the World Trade Towers.* New York: Half Pipe, In 2003.

I, Was. *A Kid, More or Less. Youtube Wasn't Around Then and the Only Streaming Sites I Knew of Were for Porn or Funny Pictures and Videos.* Sec: 4, Par:38 Subsection: 22 - There Was No Online ISBS: 9/11 Conspiracy Films or. New York, Simon and Shush, 1963.

Material, Around. *At Least None That I Had Ever Come Across.* In Fact, Pp: 108. I'd Never Even Heard of, Pp. 87. - Much Less Contemplated, Pp.1004. - The Notion of Government Involvement in 9/11. New York, Shush Simon, 1996.

The, Only. *Other Time I Had Been to the Area Before Was Two Years Earlier.* I Went With my Bro. Vol. 3 - When I Was Pitching the Magazine to Barnes & Noble. ISBS: 0983PIU787 - The Grid Was a Warzone and the Pit Was Still Smouldering. New York: Shhh, 1980.

What, I'm. *Trying to Say is That I Wasn't There Because I Was Some Psychotic Conspiracy Nut Job.* Episode: 08. Rather, I Was a Nut Job Episode: 09. Who Wound Up There Because He Was Walking in a Psychotic State From a Friend's Place – Vol. 98. New York: Simon Dithers, 1922.

A, Mere. *2,500 feet away. *Months Later I Stumbled on the Conspiracy Material.* (1890-1884). I Analysed the Counter Evidence and Debated it Extensively; Word Up Magazine back issue: 0098. I Even Made a Presentation in an Advertising Course That 9/11 had. New York: Uncensored Internet, 1995.

Government, Involvement. *The Only Reasonable Doubt I've Ever Been Able to Convince Myself of, or Anyone Else.* Issues 11-19. Is That the Government Knew an Attack of Some Kind Was on the. Chicago: Blackhawks Baby, 2010.

Way, And. *That's a Provable Assertion Derived From the Bin Laden Determined to Attack Inside U.S.* Sec: 18 Par: 18 Subsection: 83. Memo. Men's Hockey: Canada Gold, 2010.

Would, It. *Surprise Me if People Within a Government Let it Happen?* No; Groups. (1898) Of Power Always Have (1287) Sociopathic Individuals Within Them. Los Angeles: Brain Implants, 2002.

Do, I. *Believe a Government Orchestrated it All?* No; the Will and Desire for the Events Like That Day Have Been. Vol. 8-9. *Expressed and Evident in Extreme Muslim Factions for Decades.* New York: Fi Dulla Umbwella!, 1376.

Two, Years. *After the Buildings Went Down, the Scene Was Even More Ominous.* There Were Large Construction Rigs Lighting. Vol. 9367 up the excavation. Vermont. The Sidewalks Were Too Clean For New York; New York: Umbwella Fi Dulla!, 1377.

Too, New. *There Wasn't Any Passing Traffic; Not Even the Odd Cab Ramming Through Potholes Well Over the Limit.* I Walked Around. Issues: 47-48 (1997): To The East Side Of The Site Where I Came Across (some signs) exhibiting: New York: 6 Train Is Where Da Pussy @, 2005.

The, History. *Of the Site and the Two Buildings.* As I Looked Up at Them Something Happened That Only. (a person who's been on) Vol. 87. Mushrooms or acid can relate pp.98. to. *Little specs of light, as if it were*: Miami: Los Angeles w/o the Tax, 1827.

Christmas, Flowed. *Over the Boards. What Happened Next is Completely Fucked.* I - New Orleans: Great Crawfish, 2007.

Lost, Control. *Over my Mind and Something Else Took Hold and Began to Read the Story Boards to me.* (1988). No language was used, (just understanding) ISBS: 987GJJ363... language was bypassed with some strange and. San Francisco: Rollerblading With Ski Poles, 1979.

Beautiful, Telepathy. *That Was So Clear and Concise Yet Convoluted and Confounding...* Sec: 8 Par: 3 Subsection: 897 – (I can't describe.): Boston: Third World Construction Debacle, 1991.

I, Burst. *Out in a Mad Man's Laughing Fit Upon Learning the Once Grand Buildings Were Built on Landfill.* The Concept (8273-987) that the millions of (1787-1827) Vol. 32. man hours invested in the construction of the towers, was really an elaborate (effort to): Baltimore: Sounds Like Fireworks But They Aren't, 1992.

Create, More. *Landfill (in a matter of deconstructive seconds) Was Even More Hilarious.* The Fact That the Newly Destroyed Buildings (Issues: 4-44.) and human lives were then 98737-098 *hauled off to a landfill with the name of*: Las Vegas: College Fund Funded, 1950.

Fresh, Kills. *Made Me Literally Drop to My Knees at the Mercy of a Gut Wrenching Cackle.* When Act 3: Scene 12. I collected myself (and got back up to my feet the idea) 555-5555 of few thousand people dying didn't seem like a: Dallas: Ola Senior, 2000.

Big, Deal. *; according to the Reasoning That was Being Transmitted to me.* It was a Big Deal, (1986) however, because the lives Issue: 46. lost were all part of a bigger picture; they were a: Maine: Weird Writers, 1990.

Part, Of. *A Process to get Humanity Where it has to go. And then I Felt Shocked and Scared*; as Though I. Vol. 7 and 8. were in the presence (1567) of evil. And Just as I Feared for my Safety, I Stared - ISBS: 98797GHG263 - up into the sky and the: Washington D.C.: Decadent Corrupt, 2012.

Comforting, Notion. *Of "Every Evil Event in History is a Part of a Strange Fate and Destiny... Humanity is a Lump of Coal Undergoing a Series of Hardening Tragedies on the Path.* (time – time) Vol. Ect, eg, i.e. - to becoming a diamond... more perfected" came into my mind: Cleveland: Cheap Booze, 1984.

Once, That. *Sunk in I Felt Ecstatic, Free, Completely Relieved.* So Good Was the Feeling I Felt, that I Decided to Inform. Vol. 78. the world (that we're all) Pp. 89-102. on our way to perfection, *but that we had to do it*: New York: Mayor King, 2009.

Ourselves, To. *Spread the News, All I Had to Do Was Make it to Liberty St.* When I Broke Through a Couple of Revolving. (1982). doors in a (row:19 Seat: 4.) skywalk, I ended pg. 58-95. up in a large lobby area. Detroit: More Fun than Cleveland, 1923.

I, Saw. *A Sign That Pointed Towards Liberty St. I Just Had to Get Through One More Revolving Door. This door, However*, Vol. 8 & 14. wouldn't give. Pg. 37. (I put everything I had into it, but the). Austin: Legal Drugs, 2020.

Door, Was. *Firm. I Grabbed a Partition Stand and Tried Breaking Through the Glass, But, Alas, No Dice.* If That Wasn't Frustrating (1289) enough, (I soon) ISBS: 09888IHG098. realized a security guard. Austin: Legal Jug's, 2020.

Was, Yelling. *At Me. I Was Feeling so Good, so Free, so Close to Realizing Some Grandiose Vision, and Then Some Rent a Cop* row: 8 seat: 86. (had to come along) (1789) and piss on. Austin: Means Thugs, 2020.

My, Buzz. *So What Did I Do? I Did the Only Thing That Seemed Reasonable at That Particular moment.* Vol. 239. Issue: 12. Austin: Find Jobs, 2020.

I, Unbuttoned. *My Shirt and My Fly, Whipped Out My Cock, and Started Dancing Like an Indian Around a Camp Fire.* (2003) Rome: Glory Alleluia, 2003.

What, Seemed. *Like a Minute Later, About Ten Cops Showed Up Knocking* on the Other Side of the Glass Door on (1989). Liberty St. Issues:9-13. (running on almost no sleep and food for days), and. New York: 6 Train, 1997.

Weighing, About. *143 Pounds, I Knew I Didn't Stand Much of a* Chance Against Them. While Sprinting Vol. 8, 12, 18. is the one athletic Pg. 48. (ability I possess, there). New York: Hottest Women, 1997.

Was, Nowhere. *To Really Run To. So What Did I Do?* (1996). I backed away ISBS: 908098GHF987 - from them once they came inside,: New York: In Town, 1997.

Lit, Up. *A Smoke, and Proceeded to Imitate a Shootout Scene I'd Seen in a Clint Eastwood Movie,* Replete With Sound Effects; a Couple (1956). of the cops were ID: 9834. actually laughing, which made (me laugh) at the: Moscow: Never Been, 2010.

Absurdity, Of. *It All As Well. I Then Drew my Pistol and Fired on All of Them,* "Fuh-choo! Fuh-Choo! Fuh-Choo!." Vol. 23. Issue: 56. I won the Mexican Standoff - ISBS: 897UYI7 - hands down; (it wasn't even) close.: Kosovo: Another Time, 1999.

The, Only. *Problem Was My Pistol Was a Penis Manufactured in 1981.* By Then All (1989) – i.9872. of the cops were laughing and if I (had known any better I'd have been).: Toronto: Land of Nod, 1913.

Grateful, They. *Hadn't Shot or Tasered Me. Finally a Cop Came Up to Me and, In One Fell Swoop, Handcuffed* - Issue: 17. Pg. 90. – (me with one hand while) JKI:90211 - pulling up my – (pants with the other).: New Mexico: Use To Be Old, 1978.

After, Getting. Booked and Transferred From One Jail Cell to the Other, and a Couple More Reflective Sessions with The - Vol. 14 & 12. (telepathic voice) sec:89. in my head, (I wound up at Bellevue). Not soon.: New York: XO

Kitchen, 1992.

Enough, Either. *As I Almost Got Murdered in a Holding Cell* For Trying to Bum a Smoke. Back Issue: #87. Chicago: Toast, 1979.

When, You're. *Lying Down Handcuffed To a Gurney, Unequivocally Convinced That Everyone Around You is a Paid Actor* And That Everyone (1989) - you have ever (pg.83.) known or seen in life.: Toronto: Gio Ranna's, 2001.

Were, All. *Paid Actors... You Start to Feel Very Alone, Very Small, And Come to Know What the Guy Who* – (coined the word mortified) sec:8 row:6 seats: 8-10. Probably - felt like.: Miami: Geeky Golfer Orgy, 2009.

During, The. *Experience That Compelled Him to Devise Such a Word. And When You Finally Realize* That You're Not Dreaming and That. - you're.: New York: Say New York-New York 5 Times Really Fast, 1998.

Fucking, Nut's. *And In a Psyche Ward... You Realize You're In The Middle of a Nightmare.* The Three Things I. (1256). think everyone would fear – pp. 68. (being the most in life is a murderer), a pedophile, or a nutcase. New Jersey: Wrong Exit, 2007.

Some, People. *Get All Three Or a Combo of Them. Most People, Fortunately, Get None of These Roles. For me, (1632) I pulled the latter* Issue: #18. of the cards. When I realized it, all I could do was turn to my side, as far as the cuffs would allow,: New York: Crazy Cabbies, 1998.

And, Cry. *It Wasn't My Fault, My Desire, or Anything I Deserved.* Just Fucking Life. I've Been – Vol. 34. severely (depressed in life, but) pp. 71. at that moment... (existence felt like a torture session; the psychological) 1991. torturing equivalent of savage physical.: Seattle: Suicide Statistics, 2003.

Medieval, Dungeon. *Torture. Add On the Fatigue, Desire And Inability to Smoke, the Realizations That One Day We May Engineer Our* - DNA (to live forever) Issues: 7-8. with the additional backup of being able to upload our memories onto – (servers in case our bodies die) ISBS: 987227YHT9782 - (the the memories can be implanted into another grown body).: New York: Make It, 2012.

The, Experience. Of Knowing Real Dehydration and Thirst For the First Time

MAX Gin Life and, Well, it Was Just Awful. As Mercy (1928) Pg.: 2. let me begin – ibid. 139. (to slip away and part from) myself, the telepathic force returned: ISBS: 82827USWE2836 - and nudged me awake to stare at the ceiling.: Denver: Low Altitude, 2007.

It, Told. *Me That God and the Devil Hate Each Other.* God Has Rules Misunderstood by Those Who Made Them and the – Vol. 18. Cairo: Useless Rocks, 1997.

Devil, Tries. *To Make Us Break Those Rules.* But If We Can Live Life Without Hurting Each Other On Our Terms, Then God (1902) - and the devil – (don't matter anymore.) Sec:8 Seat:5 - And only then will we be free. Then I smiled, pissed myself, and fell fast asleep.: New York: 1st Avenue, 2003.

Personally, I. *Place God and the Devil In The Same Category as Santa Clause, But It made Sense at the Time.* A While Later I Awoke to See my father at my side. He was (1981) - smiling with his hand on my – issue:10: - - head. He showed me some pictures of family, told me he loved me, and (1876) reassured me that he'd get me out... *like any loving father would if they could.*: North Pole: South Pole, 1999.

And, Now. *You Should Know Why There's a Book titled,* "Don't Judge a Dick by It's Foreskin." : New York: The Big Apple, Safe To Eat?

CPSIA information can be obtained at www.ICGtesting.com
Printed in the USA
LVOW10*0734220515

439475LV00005B/7/P

9 780692 011171